Introduction

Wouldn't it feel amazing to achieve financial freedom? Never again would you have to scramble or worry about the panic that hits when your car conks out or a kitchen appliance breaks down. Once you've reached that point, you will understand what I mean. If not, then let's set you up so you are no longer living on that precipice.

The recent pandemic has affected millions of people worldwide and left many of them without the stability of a steady income, making the issue of having a financial safety net more pressing than ever. But not having to worry about covering the costs of emergencies is only one part of financial freedom. Looking ahead happily to retirement, having the flexibility to quit your unfulfilling day job or letting go of stress about the monetary impact of your every decision also come with financial independence.

A great way to achieve such freedom is by investing in Airbnb properties and becoming a host on this reputable rental platform. If you chose this book, you have probably heard the buzz about Airbnb. You have maybe even stayed a host's property or at least thought about it. It is a short-term rental phenomenon that has conquered the world. And it is still growing.

This book will show you what it means to be an Airbnb host and what responsibilities come with accommodating guests. It will show you how you can generate enough cash to buy your first property, then guide you through the steps of purchasing the property in the right location for maximum profit potential. It will also give you some important facts about Airbnb, based on the author's personal stories throughout the text. Based on episodes of the Airbnb Investment Properties Podcast, **this book will answer all of the questions you might have before jumping into investing in Airbnb** properties, and even some vital ones that have yet to cross your mind. The only thing left in the end is for you to go out and find the right property where you can invite guests and begin your journey to financial freedom.

100 Tricks to

Make Money with Airbnb

What Every Successful Vacation Rental Host Needs to Know and Do

David Leroux

About the author

David Leroux is a real estate investor, focusing exclusively on identifying high-return Airbnb properties. Born and raised in France, he trained as an engineer then decided to invest in real estate at age 25.

While keeping his 9-to-5 job, he searched for properties that he could rent out via Airbnb, recognizing that they have a much higher profitability than other investment properties. When he sought information about how to accomplish this goal, David found few resources. Over time, he developed his own method to systematically identify properties that would generate more than 20 percent cash-on-cash return to the tune of $100,000-plus in revenue per apartment. He focused on properties that could be legally rented all year-long on Airbnb and found other ways to grow his income exponentially.

He now owns more than 15 properties in five different parts of the world and quickly earned "Super Host" status on Airbnb.

Upon reaching financial freedom, he decided to coach hundreds of students who have experienced similar successes. In 2017, he created Cash Flow Street and made his teachings available globally on the leading learning platform Teachable, launching the first step-by-step easy-to-follow method to buy or rent and sub-lease Airbnb investment properties.

David's new purpose in life is to teach people how to accelerate their path to financial freedom using Airbnb properties so they can retire in fewer than three years. You can join him on this path by following the advice he shares in the next nine chapters.

Table of Contents

3: Buying your first property

16) What are the first steps to buying an Airbnb property?

17) What are three things to avoid when buying an Airbnb property?

18) How do you get the list of Airbnb properties to buy?

19) How do you buy a "legal" Airbnb property?

20) Where are the most profitable Airbnb properties?

21) What is the average amount of money needed to buy an Airbnb investment property?

22) How much money do you need to buy your first property?

23) Where can you buy an Airbnb investment property with $100,000?

24) Should you buy a small or a large Airbnb property?

25) Should you buy a single unit or a multiunit apartment?

26) Should you invest in a condo or single-family home?

27) What is the right size of an Airbnb property?

28) How do you buy Airbnb properties without worrying about the cities' Airbnb regulations?

29) Which foreign country is best suited for Airbnb investment properties?

30) What are the best markets for Airbnb investment right now?

31) Should you buy a $50,000 or $500,000 Airbnb investment property?

32) Should you buy an Airbnb near big tourist attractions only?

33) Should you buy or rent and sub-lease an Airbnb property?

34) What are the benefits if you rent (then sub-lease) an Airbnb property?

35) How do you finance an Airbnb property?

36) Which lender should you contact to finance your Airbnb investment property?

37) Is it possible to buy an Airbnb without a down payment?

38) Where can you buy a vacation rental with only $10,000 in your bank account?

39) Should you buy an Airbnb property at an auction?

40) Are there 'turnkey' Airbnb investment properties?

4: Setting yourself up for business success

41) What is a good ROI for an Airbnb investment property?

42) Should you avoid cities with Airbnb regulations?

43) Is San Diego a good market for buying Airbnb investment properties?

44) How to find out if short-term rentals are allowed from the homeowners' association?

45) Should you have a property with or without a homeowner's association (HOA)?

46) How do you manage Airbnb properties remotely?

47) Should you hire a property management company?

7: Welcoming and managing your guests

8: Ramping up your return on investment

84) Why should you focus on a financial metric other than your Airbnb revenue?

85) What ROI can you expect from a vacation rental?

86) How do you price your Airbnb to maximize revenue?

87) Is a 100% occupancy rate good or bad for your Airbnb listing?

88) What are the two critical things in your Airbnb listings that really need your attention?

89) Can you use the Airbnb Cash Flow Method to invest in Airbnb properties overseas?

90) Should you invest $100,000 in upgrading your current Airbnb or buy a new Airbnb property?

91) What is Airbnb Plus?

92) What are the top 3 smart products for your Airbnb?

93) How can you easily increase your Airbnb revenue by 10 to 50 percent with one easy-to-use tool?

94) How can you use 'ring doorbell' monitoring to increase your Airbnb revenue by 10 percent?

95) What are two tips to maximize your Airbnb tax return?

96) How can you increase your Airbnb revenue by 342 percent?

9: Looking ahead to future trends and decisions

97) What is the office rental market potential for Airbnb?

98) When will Airbnb become a publicly traded company?

99) What is an Airbnb sabbatical?

100)   What is the best exit strategy for this type of investment?

Chapter 1: What you need to know before you invest

You likely have endless questions – maybe even 100 of them -- about this type of business and if it right for you. Let's begin with why it's better than a regular job, in terms of lifestyle and financial results. You will also learn how it differs from monthly or annual rentals, while getting to know more about the risks and potential pitfalls to avoid, based on my experience.

1) Why is Airbnb better than the rat race?

As I was coming back from a dinner one day, I walked by a gym and I saw several of folks running on treadmills. I love going to the gym -- don't get me wrong -- but just a glimpse of dozens and dozens of people on the treadmills, while staying at the same place, put a different mental picture in my head. It made me think of how most employees are working so hard, literally sweating at work and not going anywhere fast in terms of savings. They are running so that one day they can have the financial freedom to get off that treadmill and do the things that they love. I see this, especially where I live in Silicon Valley and the San Francisco Bay area. Maybe you have also realized that so many people feel stuck.

I was there five years ago. Working in my day job, I wanted to do something else with my life. I wanted to have more free time, so I just decided to get off the "treadmill" or the rat race for three seconds and start investing so I could earn some passive income. I am not saying Airbnb is the only way to go, but that's the way I chose. When I started trying to make some extra income on the side, I wasn't very successful with my first property because no one guided me. Regardless, it was a necessary step to see a different path than the rat race -- that treadmill of just going to the gym every day, going to the same company every day, and being stuck in one place.

I invested in one property, then a second and a third. I started to see that I got better ideas in terms of choosing the right properties. As a result, I started to earn more profits as I managed my properties better. I could see the nightly rates increasing, started at $1,000 a month, then $2,000, then $5,000 extra income a month until I earned *my* financial freedom. My key message from this is that it is okay to not invest in Airbnb. Choose your own passive income stream, but please don't stay stuck in the rat race.

Take that very first step down from this treadmill, beyond your day to day job. Take that first important step to create this extra income for yourself and focus on it so you get better and better at it. If it is Airbnb investment property, great. If it is a multi-family property, great. If you want to go into some other financial assets, great, but be ultra-focused and commit to taking serious action steps to create the financial freedom that you deserve.

2) Why should you invest in this type of rental?

You might be asking yourself why would you choose a property for short-term rentals? There are both financial and non-financial benefits.

When it comes to money, people renting a property as an Airbnb generate on average three times more profit than while renting the same property with a standard one-year lease. That is three times more money for you and your future. Airbnb properties are also very profitable in terms of investment. They can generate more than 40 percent return when you know where to buy them. Another financial bonus is the tax benefit that is tied to all investment properties. You will learn more about these later in this book.

Now when it comes to the non-financial benefits, the most obvious one is that now you have a vacation home anytime you need it. You can just block the days you will be using the property for yourself and enjoy a holiday in your own vacation home. You will also have a great opportunity to network with guests from all around the world, get to know different cultures and learn from them.

3) What are the basic Do's and Don'ts for first-time Airbnb investor?

Don't do it alone. Don't buy a property without any advice from an Airbnb property investment coach. If you don't have one, you can register for my free workshop at cashflowstreet.com.

Don't overspend. Whether it is on buying the property itself or the furniture, do not spend too much money and dig yourself into a financial hole. Cashflow is important. For instance, you need to think about the number of people that can sleep in your property based on the number of rooms and bathrooms, rather than the square footage of your property. The size does not generate cash flow; the number of beds does.

Don't communicate with your guests on your own. Hire a team of professionals that will do that for you. A virtual assistant can check your guests in, send a welcome message, contact the plumber to deal with any plumbing issues, etc. You need to focus *your* time finding new properties to invest in.

Do get an interior designer (if you are not talented in this area). Photos sell so you need to make sure that your place looks good. Don't assume you can do it on your own if you can't.

Do get a professional photographer. As I already said, photos are key to promotion, so you need to make sure you have the best images possible in your listing.

Do use an automatic pricing tool. Don't try to price it yourself. Many online tools are easy to use and can increase your profit.

4) What are the differences between Airbnb investment properties other real-estate properties?

The main difference between an Airbnb investment property and any other real estate property is that Airbnb is three times more profitable on average than long-term lease property. That means you can accelerate your cash flow and get your financial freedom much faster than with any other property investment.

Another advantage of Airbnb property is that you stay there for your vacation. Simply block the dates in the calendar on the site and you can spend a nice relaxing holiday there.

The third benefit is that you can have a tax deduction for a vacation destination at your Airbnb property. If you set up your Airbnb as a business and you spend more than half of the time there doing business, you can deduct the necessary expenses. Always consult with a specialist in the area where your property is located so you can take advantage of tax loopholes legally.

Also, consider the property's appreciation, meaning the equity increase of the asset as a benefit. You also use its depreciation as an expense to help you with your tax return.

Last, but not least, thanks to Airbnb you will get to meet many people from all around the world, which can help you grow your network.

5) Why do Airbnb investment properties generate three times more profits than traditional real estate investment?

I was asking myself this question when I was first starting. Would I make more money with an Airbnb? Should I invest in vacation rentals versus the more traditional real estate? The more traditional rentals sounded easier, you find a tenant and sign it over for a long-term lease. So why bother with short-term rentals? The only way I would bother is if I made much more money without more headaches and stress. Those were the two main things for me when I started.

But I did not know how to evaluate properties. I did not know which ones generate more money, because to be clear, not all investments in Airbnb make money. You must know how to filter the right ones based on the demand, whether there are targeted at tourists and whether the property is in the right location.

In my case and I decided to jump in and buy my first property, then my second and third and so on. I could then quickly navigate and see what the top 1 percent of the most profitable properties are and generate more profit for myself.

But having a property in the right location is not the only thing that is important to make money with Airbnb. You need to make sure that you do not have a property management company. This is especially important. They will take your profit and you would be in the same spot as if you were in a traditional real estate. Instead of having a property management company have your team with a virtual assistant, cleaning service, plumber and so on.

These are the two main things - buying in the right location and having no property management company to take money out of your pockets. When you fulfill these two conditions, you are going to cash out profitably each month with your Airbnb properties.

6) What are the risks of Airbnb investing?

As with every investment, there are certain risks that you cannot avoid. But as Warren Buffet said, "Risk is not knowing what you are doing." So, if you are aware of what you are doing, you can reduce and control the inevitable risks.

When it comes to Airbnb investment properties, there are two main types of risks: profit risk and personal liability risk.

The profit risk is mainly due to three factors: a city's Airbnb regulations, so make sure that you buy property in the right area where you *can* operate as an Airbnb; the documentation with the Homeowners association, if there is one, so you can rent your place to vacationers; and assessment to ensure you are buying a property in a location with high demand and low supply.

For controlling the personal liability risk, you need to make sure that you have short-term rental insurance, specialized for Airbnb properties. You can take other steps, which will be described in more detail later.

7) What are the top 3 Airbnb investment tips?

There are many different tricks on how to maximize the profit from Airbnb property investment. I am going to share with you the top 3 that I discovered over the years.

1. **Select the best location** – This is essential in maximizing your profit. Do not buy a place just because it is close to you. You can easily manage a property that is outside of your town, but you need to make sure that it is in a high-demand location where it is legal to operate an Airbnb. I have a whole chapter on this in my workshop Airbnb Cash Flow Method.

2. **Have a great listing** – This is especially important during low season as only the listings with the best description and best photos get booked. The photos convince people to choose your listing so they must be outstanding.

3. **Be a pricing ninja** – Don't worry, you do not need to do this on your own. Many great tools can help you set the right price every single day. You can use Pricelabs, Wheelhouse or Beyond Pricing. Airbnb has also its tool for dynamic pricing, but there is still room for improvement, and it does not compare to the three mentioned before.

8) What are the top 3 Airbnb investment properties mistakes to avoid?

To generate the most profit possible and maximize the revenue, there are some traps or mistake you will want to avoid. These are the top 3:

1. Not being aware of the current and future **Airbnb risks in the zoning** where you want to operate. In other words, this means that you need to make sure that you are in the right zoning where it is okay to operate Airbnb year-round without limitations. There are plenty of them, you just need to inform yourself properly

2. Not being able to **assess the profit accurately.** This is something dear to my heart as I have developed a calculator to predict the future profitability of property before you even buy it. Do not buy a property without confidently knowing what your profit will be.

3. Spending **too much time managing**. Once you own a property, it might be tempting to communicate with guests and answer all their questions, some might even want you to be their concierge and schedule their activities. You might even think of cleaning yourself to save some money. Please don't do it. It takes too much time. You should always outsource these responsibilities to make sure you are as efficient as possible.

Now that you have a sense of some of the decisions you have ahead, let's look at how Airbnb enriches lives for me, its CEO and my accountant. Hopefully, it will inspire you to join us.

Chapter 2: Background on the Airbnb business

Before we go any further, it will be helpful for you to get more insight into the scope and potential of this company and your possible role as an investor.

9) How did you get your start with Airbnb properties?

People often ask me how it all started for me, before I started making more than $1 million a year with my properties. Let me tell you a short story about the time when I got very scared after losing my job while having almost nothing in the bank. That might help you understand my journey.

After losing the job, I had difficulty finding a new one that paid as well. As a result, I decided I should buy some real estate to earn some income on the side in hopes of one day reaching financial independence. At that time, I have heard from a friend that Airbnb properties could be quite a lucrative investment. I was intrigued. But I was also struggling with not having enough money for the down payment to buy a property and to find a property that would be profitable. I was getting more nervous about my financial situation and overwhelmed by the world on real-estate investment, as it was new for me.

I decided to rent a room in my home via the Airbnb platform so I could get familiar with it and generate money for the down payment to buy a property, which went well. After that, I did quick research myself and bought my first Airbnb property. However, I made the mistake of not looking up city regulations beforehand and only found out afterward that I could only rent it out for 90 days out of the whole year. If I went over that limit, I could be evicted and ordered to pay a pretty high fee. By being limited to renting 90 days of the year, I was losing money. Instead of generating passive income, I was draining my savings more and more each month. It was a scary and dark period for me.

But I was not ready to give up on my dream of Airbnb property investment yet. I decided to change my approach to a more systematic one. I developed a step-by-step technique to find the most profitable Airbnb properties that can be rented year-round without worrying about regulations. The moment I figured this out, everything changed for me. I was able to convince landlords to rent their properties long-term then allow me to sub-lease them. I found the top one percent of profitable properties, which was a game-changer. I was also able to identify properties in zonings where Airbnb is legal, even if it is not in other parts of the city. Thanks to this systematic method, I was able to create an investment tool that can be used again and again. I increased my income exponentially and reached financial freedom.

More importantly, I was able to spread my message and make a difference in other people's lives. I can live my dream with Airbnb property investment, without having to worry about money again.

That is why I am so passionate about this business and my Airbnb Cash Flow Method.

10) How big is Airbnb?

Airbnb is a phenomenon for guests, for hosts and for the hotel industry. It has more than seven million listings -- that's seven million places all over the world, with about 80 percent of them outside of the United States. Many of them are in cities in Europe, especially in Paris, Barcelona and similar tourist destinations. Airbnb's bed count is higher than the top five international hotel brands combined. If you realize that the number of all the rooms of the Marriott, Intercontinental, Hilton, Accor and Wyndham are lower than the number of Airbnb listings, you can see how big this phenomenon is. As you know, Airbnb (starting in 2007) is much younger than those brands, which have been around for decades. So, it has millions of listings and growing.

You may be thinking that it is not growing as fast anymore. Well, think again. Just in the U.S. alone, the number of listings is growing by 45 percent year to year. That is massive. It is a significant amount of increase and it is not stopping anytime soon. The financial performances are excellent for Airbnb and the total number of users all over the world for those seven million listings is now more than 150 million.

This is the scale of Airbnb today. And that is why so many people are making money from it. Many hosts begin by just renting a room in their current homes, then scale up with additional properties because there is a need. People want to feel like a local. People want to have a different experience than they get with the hotel industry. And we still see massive growth ahead for the short-term rental industry.

11) What is the most popular Airbnb property in the world?

You may be thinking it is in Paris or in a city with a booming economy. Could it be somewhere in China or maybe in Bali because it is just so popular on Airbnb? These places have a lot of cute Airbnbs that people from all over the world want to see.

However, the most popular Airbnb in the world is a tiny cabin called the Mushroom Dome Retreat located in Aptos, California. If you type *mushroom dome, Airbnb Aptos, California* in the Google search bar, you can see exactly how this place looks like. It is, in fact, a very tiny property. It looks like a mushroom dome and it has a high factor of cuteness. Only three people can sleep there, so you cannot have too many guests. If you ask me, it must be cramped. But it is a cabin in the middle of the woods. It has beautiful triangular windows, through which you can watch the sky. I am sure it is very romantic from the bed.

What I am trying to emphasize is that people are looking for places that are unique. It must be charming, but it does not have to be huge. In fact, the smaller places are more popular. This is where you make the best return on investment as well.

So, do not try to get a big place just to impress your guests. If you did, you would have more space to fill with furniture, which would cost a lot of money. Go small to go big.

This mushroom dome is the perfect example of that.

12) What is Airbnb CEO's morning routine?

What does Airbnb CEO Brian Chesky do every morning? He has an extremely specific, simple and effective twist on the standard to-do list. Chesky explained his technique to Greylock investor, LinkedIn founder, and Airbnb board member Reid Hoffman in an episode on Hoffman's podcast *Masters of Scale*. Here is what Brian Chesky does every morning.

First, he creates a list of everything he wants to accomplish that day and strives to make it as exhaustive as possible. This means everything. Then he groups similar tasks. This grouping is particularly important because then he tries to find one action that can take care of all the tasks in one group. It is like a game of leverage. Is there one action in each of those groups that can cover all these tasks? Then he repeats the grouping and refines the process until he has only a few big tasks.

Hopefully his not-so-secret morning routine can inspire you to do more in your day.

13) Is Marriott becoming a significant competitor of Airbnb?

You have read it in the previous parts of this book, Airbnb is massive in its reach. With more than seven million listings, Marriott Hotels is a tiny company in terms of the number of listings and the number of rooms that they have in comparison. Unsurprisingly, Marriott looks at Airbnb and thinks about how they could get a piece of this growing market. So, they try to launch some set of homes that would compete with Airbnb.

But what is the key aspect of Airbnb? You feel more like at home or like a local. The Airbnb and Marriott experience are vastly different. Marriott now tries to blur the line since they want so badly to go into the Airbnb market.

Meanwhile, Airbnb also wants to get into the hotel market. They launched Airbnb Plus, where hosts must meet several requirements to be a part of this unique category. That part of Airbnb is becoming more standardized while the company also has a section with boutique hotels.

You can see that the lines are getting blurry from both sides. But I am not worried that Marriott is coming into the Airbnb space because its brand is so established, and it does not have the infrastructure for Airbnb. It is also going to take quite some time for it to grow their pool of listings on Airbnb. The last time I checked, there were around 2,000 Marriott properties, they call them homes and villas, that compete with the seven million-plus listings on Airbnb. Airbnb is still on top with the brand recognition for this type of vacation rentals.

14) Is there a Netflix movie about Airbnb?

Yes, there is. It is a 2019 movie entitled *Wine Country* that takes place in Napa. Tina Fey portrays the Airbnb host. It is a feel-good comedy about the power of friendship, reminding me of Saturday Night Live. On RottenTomatoes.com, the users ranked it at about 65 to 67 percent so it is an okay movie. It's not a blockbuster but a fun light movie to watch if you want to relax but still be in the world of Airbnb.

In a different category, but still on Netflix, about Airbnb, there is the documentary *Stay here* which I highly recommend. You can get plenty of tips on how to set up your Airbnb by quality hosts.

Airbnb storylines are slowly coming to Netflix, but it is also testing out its video-streaming platform. The company has not released it yet. Will Airbnb become the new Netflix? We will see.

15) How did the author's accountant become his main Airbnb competitor?

Every year, like most of you, I do my tax return. Typically, I sit down with my accountant at the end of January. We have developed a great relationship over the years. He has around 120 other clients. Because of his work, he can see my taxes and assets in great detail, especially my Airbnb properties. He can see all the properties I have in California, Hawaii, Florida, etc. He has access to all the details about my investments, not just where they are, but also the return on investment which is anywhere from 20 to 40-plus percent, depending on the property. Those are very appealing types of assets of investment.

He realized that this is very profitable and attempted to copy that type of investment. He also decided to take my online course, the Airbnb Cash Flow Method. He looked at properties that are in the same building and started scaling his own small Airbnb empire.

Each year we joke about him being my main competitor. In reality, I am incredibly happy for him and his very profitable side business. I am also happy to have shared this knowledge with him and that I am also able to share my Airbnb investment method with you.

Chapter 3: Buying your first property

Now it's time to get down to the details of how to get your hands on your first property so you can begin your own journey. Maybe you will ease into it with a sub-lease or jump right in with a purchase. There is a lot to cover, in terms of zoning, financing and sourcing the right property.

16) What are the first steps to buying an Airbnb property?

1. **Plan.** You need to assess your current financial situation and passive income, then set your goal and figure out how much income you need to get there. This will help you determine what type of Airbnb property you need so that you can fulfill your desired objective.

2. **Buy**. Assess which area to buy the property so that it complies with the Airbnb regulations in the city where the property is located, but also so that it is profitable, so you can earn as much as possible. You need to, therefore, know how to identify the top one per cent of the Airbnb properties in your area. In this step, you also need a strategy for financing the investment. For this, you need a bank that specializes in short-term rentals and can help you find the best solution for your specific situation.

3. **Profit**. You need to make sure you generate as much profit as possible. For that, you need to have the best listing that will differentiate your property from the competition. A great team of people to manage your property for the right price is also essential in this step. And the last thing you need in the profit step is to have the right insurance so that your property, your revenue and your liability are covered.

Following these three steps will generate a great cashflow. This is also something I teach in more detail in my free workshop that you can check on cashflowstreet.com.

17) What are three things to avoid when buying an Airbnb property?

1. **Do not guess the city regulations** – You might have heard the news about New York or Los Angeles regulating Airbnb rentals. Yes, some places regulate this industry and it is great news for you, as this practice limits the supply. Most people do not understand this but when you know exactly where to find a property in the right legal zoning within a regulated city, you have a gold mine. This is one of the best-kept secrets. But you cannot just guess the regulations, you need to do your homework and find out where it is okay and where not.

2. **Do not guess the profitability of the property** - There are tools you can use to find out the precise

profitability of property for short-term rentals. I provide one such tool in my Cash Flow Method, however, you can find other similar tools for this purpose. Just be sure that you use something specific for short-term rental that other experienced investors use.

3. **Do not buy too far** – This is especially important if you are buying your first property. Try to buy within a one-hour drive from where you live, so that you can get on-site fast in case you are needed. This does not apply for your second or third property, but with the first one, try to stay close to home so you can have a bit more control and learn properly from this initial investment.

18) How do you get the list of Airbnb properties to buy?

You might be tempted to ask this question; however, it is not the right approach. You would get the fish without learning how to catch fish yourself. What you want to do is build the skills to evaluate properties so you can get to them first. If there would be a list of great properties available, there would be too much competition. You can see this in the more traditional real estate. With family homes, for instance, it is not unusual to have 20-plus offers for one property. This does not happen with Airbnb because there is no such list.

It is key to identify how to find those properties yourself and quickly. Firstly, you need to educate yourself about the zoning in your particular city and see where the right areas are and which the ones to avoid. You also need to have a blueprint to assess the profitability of the properties, which will give you the answer whether to invest or not.

These are the two aspects to focus on when you are deciding where to invest. I also talk about these tips in more detail my Airbnb Cash Flow Method where I share my secrets about how to assess these properties fast.

19) How do you buy a "legal" Airbnb property?

This is one of the first questions that probably crosses the mind of anyone thinking of dipping their toes into Airbnb property investment. "Legal" in this context means a property that can be operated 365 days a year without the fear of someone from the city knocking on the door one day, saying you cannot rent the property out as an Airbnb. There are many places where this is not allowed, however, there are also many places where it is perfectly okay.

Here are the three best tips on how to find the right (and legal) Airbnb properties:

1. **Do your homework about the county zoning –** Make sure that you are looking at properties only in the zones where this type of rental is allowed, to save

yourself time and money. The information is publicly available from the planning department.

2. **Check the city rules about Airbnb** – Big cities typically have some restrictions in place, but smaller places might have some as well. So, make sure you are up to date on the ordinance of your city

3. **Read up on the Covenants, Conditions & Restrictions (CC&R) of the property before placing any offer** –From this document, it will be clear whether that particular property can be operated as an Airbnb or whether it is prohibited.

20) Where are the most profitable Airbnb properties?

Every investor wants to make the most of each property. The question now arises where to buy THE properties that will make me the most money. There are three things to look for when seeking the right cash-flow-friendly property:

1. **Places that have a lot of tourists AND business travelers** – Renting to business travelers is on the rise, so find a place where you can capitalize on both. Tourists and business travelers make for a magic combination.

2. **Properties with kick-ass amenities** – Just imagine how much revenue nice listing photos with a pool and a hot tub can bring. These amenities do not have to be

directly in the apartment you are renting but focus your search on a complex where these are available.

3. **The right supply-and-demand ratio** – Ideally, look for a property in a city or county with a lot of Airbnb restrictions, but within the legal zoning and rules. This will limit your competitors, raising the chances of guests choosing your property.

21) What is the average amount of money needed to buy an Airbnb investment property?

To buy a property, typically you would need 20 to 40 percent of the purchase price as the down payment. It could also be a bit more, depending on your particular situation. Nowadays, it does not get lower than 20 percent. The approximate purchase price of investment properties is around $300,000 to $700,000.

On top of that, you also need to set up your place with furniture, equipment, towels, etc. The price of that will depend on the type of place you have. If it is a studio, it will cost around $3,000, for a one-bedroom apartment it is around $5 000, and for two-bedroom around $7,000.

Now let's do the math. Let's assume that you are buying a one-bedroom apartment to accommodate four people, using one bedroom plus a sofa bed for two people. You would need a down payment of 25 percent of $500,000 (an average value of such property), which is $125,000, plus $5,000 for the set-up, plus the closing and the prepaid items such as interest and property taxes. This would amount to around $138,000, which is an average amount of money to buy an Airbnb property.

22) **How much money do you need to buy your first property?**

Firstly, you do not need to immediately buy a property. It is possible to rent and sub-lease a property as an Airbnb listing, within legal zoning. This is great for beginners who might not yet have the down payment to invest in their own property.

If you are, however, ready to invest, typically you would need between 20 to 40 percent of the purchase price of the property as a down payment. As with any other mortgage, the exact amount would depend on the bank, the property and its zoning, your finances, etc.

23) **Where can you buy an Airbnb investment property with $100,000?**

You have a $100,000 that you want to invest in an Airbnb investment property. That is amazing, but now you need to know where to buy such property.

Firstly, you need to identify the cost of setting up and closing a vacation rental. For $100,000, you should consider around $20,000 for both costs. Banks typically want 30 percent of the purchase price of the investment property as a down payment, and you now have $80,000 that you can use as this down payment. This means you can buy property for $266,666.

Secondly, you need to assess where in the U.S. or the elsewhere in the world where you can buy an Airbnb property. There are two criteria for that - the zoning of the place you want to buy allows you to operate an Airbnb 365 days a year and the area is highly profitable. Do not buy a property in a place where no one wants to come, even if this type of rental is allowed there.

If you need help pinpointing specific cities where to buy an Airbnb investment property, feel free to look at my quarterly report of the best cities for Airbnb property investment or simply look at my Airbnb Cash Flow Method for additional guidance.

24) Should you buy a small or a large Airbnb property?

When you are trying to find the best property, deciding whether to buy a smaller unit with a smaller down payment or a five-bedroom family house with a larger down payment is probably one of the first things that you will need to do.

In Airbnb's return on investment, the size matters. You always want to buy a smaller property to make more profit for the money you put in. If you buy a studio or one-bedroom apartment you will have a better return on investment than if you buy a large family home in the same neighborhood.

In my case, for example, I currently have 16 properties that are either studio or a one-bedroom apartment. Each time I was considering investing in a two- or three-bedroom apartments, the ROI was not as good as with the smaller units.

Also, having smaller units gives you fewer headaches, is easier to manage and maintain and comes with lower risk. Also, if you have a good and efficient team of cleaners and people responsible for checking guests in and out, you can have one guest checking out at 11 a.m., cleaners cleaning the place for four hours (which is more than enough for a smaller unit) and you can have another guest check-in that afternoon. This would not be easily done in a bigger place that takes longer to clean properly.

Smaller units are not only financially better for you as an investor, but they are also much more flexible.

25) Should you buy a single unit or a multiunit apartment?

You probably know the saying "Go big or go home." Well, it does not necessarily apply to buying an Airbnb investment property, especially if you are just starting out. When you are choosing whether to buy a single unit or a multiunit apartment complex, I always recommend a single unit for starters. Do not be overconfident and jump straight into a multiunit apartment complex with your first investment in a new market. Start with a single unit, get familiar with the area, the market, seasonality and the revenue that you can generate.

Once you know your way around the market there and what you can expect in terms of revenue, you can expand. I call it the "land and expand strategy." Make sure you land well in a new market with a small unit (studio or one-bedroom apartment) then you can scale up to a duplex or even a motel or bed and breakfast with multiple units.

26) Should you invest in a condo or single-family home?

Both properties can be great so let's look and the pros and cons of both.

The positive of buying a condo is that they are often in busy locations with many tourists and business travelers. Also, they are relatively small, typically a studio or one to two-bedroom apartments, so they are easy to set up and do not cost that much. They are easier and less stressful for you to maintain because there is the homeowner's association (HOA) that takes care or the surrounding area. The HOA can, however, also pose as a con, as you must check with them (before buying or renting the place) to see if they allow short-term rentals in the building. Another con is that you are close to the neighbors who might be sensitive to noise, so you need to check with them and manage this potentially problematic situation.

As for the single-family home, the advantage is obviously that your guests have more privacy. You are further away from the neighbors which means fewer noise issues. That still does not mean that you should let anyone in your place. You need to assess your guests, but it is more manageable with neighbors not right under your nose. On the other hand, all the maintenance is on your shoulders, whether it is yard work or a leaking roof. Also, because it is a bigger space, you will have a higher upfront payment because you must furnish the whole place.

For me, I focus first and foremost on condos. They are a great option, with less maintenance, fewer headaches and great locations.

27) What is the right size of an Airbnb property?

I recommend going for the smaller properties rather than big houses. Why? Smaller units typically have a better return on investment.

Firstly, with smaller places, you also have a smaller down payment, so it is going to be more affordable and your investment is going to be lower. Also, the set-up cost is lower for smaller units. You can imagine that if you are going for a four-bedroom house furnishing the whole place, buying linens and towels everywhere is going to be expensive.

Think also of your *return* on investment. You might think that with a bigger place you can get much more revenue. This is, however, not necessarily true. It is, for instance, better to have a one-bedroom apartment rather than two-bedroom because you earn money based on how many people can sleep in your apartment, not the square footage. In one-bedroom, you can have two people in the bedroom and two people on the sofa bed in the living room, which is quite standard and popular number of guests for Airbnb. Yes, in a two-bedroom unit, you could accommodate six guests, but this number of guests is not that common and could likely result in low occupancy rates.

So, go small to go big on the return on investment.

28) How do you buy Airbnb properties without worrying about the cities' Airbnb regulations?

You have probably heard on the news that Los Angeles, Paris or Barcelona (or other big cities) have rules and regulations for Airbnb. And if they do not have regulations yet, they soon will. However, there are ways to go around these regulations but do it perfectly legally.

What I recommend when you are investing in a big city like the ones I mentioned, do not go for a single-family home. It may sound like a good idea, but it would be a big mistake. Single-family homes are, as the name suggests, for a single family and you should not choose this type of property for vacation rentals.

Instead, choose properties in vacation rental areas. Yes, there are many vacation rental zonings even in big cities. This is one of the best-kept secrets and something I teach in the Airbnb Cash Flow method (a free course on cashflowstreet.com). When you focus on these areas, you can operate your Airbnb business legally in a city with regulations. And you also want these regulations because they limit the supply and increase your revenue.

29) Which foreign country is best suited for Airbnb investment properties?

Your level of profit depends on the demand and supply, so you want to be in a location with exceedingly high demand and low supply, but in a place where you can operate Airbnb legally year-round.

There is many a locale with high demand, like Bali in Indonesia, France or Mexico. Depending on the place, you can also have low supply compared to the demand. This can be tempting, especially if you want to buy a property somewhere where you also want to go on vacation. But you should always be extremely cautious.

Personally, I do not recommend starting your Airbnb business with a foreign property, because you need to be there to assess the local market, which is going to be difficult if it is far from home. Getting to know the market takes time and cannot be done during a few days while on vacation.

Also, you need to speak the language. Imagine buying a property in China without speaking Mandarin. Good luck trying to manage it and arrange cleaning or basic repairs. The distance would also make it challenging to set up a local team that will manage your property.

Different currencies create additional risk and responsibility that you probably want to avoid. There are plenty of great and profitable places in America that you can start.

30) What are the best markets for Airbnb investment right now?

There are tons of markets and cities to invest in and I summarize more than 90 cities in my quarterly report. Here I want to highlight the top three things that help me, and my students, assess the best markets, so you can focus on those and make them actionable.

1. It has to **be touristic** – Choose the cities or areas with the most tourism traffic.
2. **Avoid very seasonal places** – With seasonal areas, you will have a big difference in occupancy between the summer and winter. Knowledge of seasonality across the months is important.

3. Choose a **city with regulations but with legal zonings** – At first, it may sound counterintuitive, but you need an area with limited supply. Do not look at cities where you can operate Airbnb everywhere as the supply – and competition -- there would be extremely high.

31) Should you buy a $50,000 or $500,000 Airbnb investment property?

As everything in investment, the answer depends on several factors. I would suggest that you always make your decision not only based on the purchase price of the property but also two key metrics: cash flow (yes, as a Cash Flow in my Cash Flow Method) and cash on cash return.

A price of $50,000 might seem great, since you can find many properties that are this cheap in the U.S. But if they generate low cash flow, such as $100 to $200 per month, you can still lose money. You still have to set up the place and hire a team that will manage this property, whether it costs $50,000 or $100,000.

So, in this case, your cash on cash return would be great but cash flow terrible and it would not be a great idea to invest in such property. To calculate this ratio, also known as an equity dividend rate, divide your initial investment by your annual before-tax income.

I always target properties with at least \$1,000 cash flow net, meaning after tax and expenses, and with at least 12 percent cash on cash return. These are the aspects of the property you need to look at besides the purchase price of the property.

32) Should you only buy an Airbnb near big tourist attractions?

Having an Airbnb near big tourist attractions, like Disneyland for example, is great, but make sure you are following all tips and guidance from my Cash Flow Method.

You should widen your focus beyond areas with tourist attractions. Although they are key drivers, be sure to find a place that also attracts business travelers as they make great guests. Also, their companies usually pay for accommodation, so they are less sensitive to pricing. Airbnb now offers a special category of hotel-like listings called Airbnb Plus which is especially fitting for business travelers, so make sure you get on that list.

Most people think that for Airbnb, there are the tourist places, the business travel places and then there are a few gold mines that appeal to both tourists and business travelers and that's it. That is wrong. There are many other great spots and landmarks which you can have a highly profitable Airbnb. Take areas beside military bases as one example. There are always a lot of families and friends coming to visit the people working and living on these bases, and they need to stay somewhere. In California, there is a base in Morena Valley, and the real estate there is quite cheap so you could find a great deal and have a fantastic investment return.

33) Should you buy or rent and sub-lease an Airbnb property?

This is an often-asked question and my answer to it is that you should do both, rent and sub-lease as well as buy.

Now, there might be a situation where you do not have a choice. If you do not have the money for the down payment, you must rent and sub-lease a property to generate cash. There are lots of opportunities where you can rent with a long-term lease under your name or the name of your limited liability company (LLC) then sub-lease it via Airbnb. On my Cash Flow Method site, you can find tips on how to convince your landlord to allow you to sub-lease the property. It can be easy to do so if you know what to say and what not to say.

If you do have the money for the down payment to buy the property, always choose this option. Why? Because you have additional taxation tools to increase your fortune if you own the property you are renting. One is the depreciation, a great tax reduction tool. The second is the appreciation of the property, so if the value of the property increases, you profit from it. So, if you can buy, do it and do not think twice.

34) What are the benefits if you rent (then sub-lease) an Airbnb property?

I generate more than $1 million in revenue with Airbnb properties, some of which I own and some of which I rent and sub-lease. Waiting until you can afford to buy will delay your entry into this business, so you must weigh that cost.

Now, you don't want to rent just any property, as you will be tied with a contract to rent this place for at least one or two years. You need to make sure that you rent a property that you can sub-lease for short-term rentals and that is in a good profitable location so that you can earn money from it.

Renting and sub-leasing a property might be a great solution for risk-averse investors. You can implement a "rent and expand" strategy – first you rent one property and once you start seeing the money, you have higher confidence in your revenue you can expand by renting or buying other property in the same area.

35) How do you finance an Airbnb property?

For many realistic investors, this is a legitimate concern as several banks might not yet recognize Airbnb revenue as income. It is always best to work with a bank that is familiar with Airbnb cash flow when you are qualifying for such property. As it is a relatively new type of investment, not all banks will have this experience. This might result in them only recognizing the property as an expense which could skew your debt-to-income ratio and make it more challenging for you to qualify.

However, you should gravitate towards banks that recognize the Airbnb income and have experience with these properties: Quicken Loans, Citizen Bank, Better Mortgage and many others.

Depending on the zoning, you would have a specific bank to help you finance your Airbnb property. The down payment varies based on the specific property, but it is typically around 30 percent of the purchase price. You might pay a bit less, or if you are at a higher risk, you might have to put down 40 percent of the price.

Also, keep in mind that the interest rates might go up, however it is always possible to negotiate and get the best financing opportunity possible. Make sure you do your homework about all possible banks and get yourself the best loan specifically for Airbnb investment properties.

36) **Which lender should you contact to finance your Airbnb investment property?**

The truth is that many banks are not familiar with Airbnb or vacation rentals, meaning short-term rentals. Wells Fargo, Bank of America, Bank of the West, Chase, you name it, will not finance your Airbnb properties.

But the good news is some lenders are much more agile. That is what I realized when I started to buy my first, second or third Airbnb property. I needed to focus on those lenders that have special programs for Airbnb properties, and that understand the profitability. They already have similar customers; have proof point; and they do not ask for a long-term lease to approve someone for a loan.

There are plenty of these other lenders, but they are specialized, and they have special loan programs. This is something that I teach my students in the Cash Flow Method so that they can get to this lender list quickly, talk to the right financial partner and get the loan as quickly as possible.

37) Is it possible to buy an Airbnb without a down payment?

The short answer is no. Typically, you would need around 30 percent of the purchase price of the property as a down payment.

The good news is that you can generate the down payment for the property you want to invest in, by using Airbnb or similar platforms like VRBO or Booking.com. You can rent out a property under a standard one-year lease in your name, then sub-lease it as an Airbnb listing and keep the profit.

This would also be a good training for you to familiarize yourself with how operating an Airbnb works, before investing more heavily. There are five steps you need to follow if you want to generate the down payment via a sub-lease:

1. Rent a place in legal zoning or Airbnb friendly city.
2. Talk to your landlord. Do not try to hide this activity. You might want to offer paying a 10 percent higher rent and sign an agreement on paper that you can operate an Airbnb in your rental unit.
3. Do the math to make sure the place is profitable. Your rent should be lower than what you get for renting it out.
4. Have a kick-ass listing to generate as much profit as possible.
5. Repeat the steps by renting and sub-leasing multiple properties.

38) Where can you buy a vacation rental with only $10,000 in your bank account?

There is no such thing as no down payment in an investment property. You are going to need to spend a little bit of money to get a loan and finance the property. But the good news is that in the U.S., there is a wide range when it comes to house prices.

There are some great markets where you do not need to spend a lot of money to get a vacation rental that performs well. But to buy the property, you would need to have the down payment in your bank account, or you would need to generate this cash. If you want, you can even rent your entire apartment or home when you go on vacation for the weekend to generate this down payment.

Once you have this money, you need to figure out where are you going to invest it. There are a lot of cities out there that are pretty cheap. A down payment as low as $10,000 would get you a vacation rental, for example, in Dayton, Ohio. There are many places like this out there that perform very well on Airbnb. They may not be the typical vacation rental place that you may think about, like Florida or California, but Airbnb is literally everywhere, and people need places to stay. They often prefer to stay in an Airbnb instead of in a hotel.

As you can see, even $10,000 can get you going to build your Airbnb empire.

39) Should you buy an Airbnb property at an auction?

I was always fascinated by the auction sites. I know many people have been remarkably successful in buying the right property as-is via an auction most of the time. When you buy on auctions, typically you cannot see the property and you are going to have to do some renovation.

But when it comes to Airbnb, especially for your first properties, I do strongly believe that it is important to see the property and buy it with as little renovation as possible. Some of you may love to renovate. As for me, I hate it. It's additional work, it's stressful, and it takes away your time, therefore money as well. When you do the renovations, you cannot rent it, so you have a lost-opportunity cost.

Now, some websites are interesting to find very cheaper properties, and you can always look for some great opportunities there. One that I want to mention, because I have some experience with it, is called bid4assets.com. On this site, you can buy properties for $500, $1,000, or $2,000. But, as we say, you get what you pay for. You are going to end up with some properties in the middle of nowhere. But it is always worth it to check it out. Maybe there are some properties not too far from where you live. Or you want to take the risk and buy properties at that price and do just a few renovations to get them going.

I used that website about 10 years ago to buy some beautiful land. It had a unique view of three bridges in the Silicon Valley from a city called Point Richmond. To this day, I remember the view of the Golden Gate Bridge, the Richmond Bridge and the East Bay Bridge, which is very unique. I was told by the city of Richmond that I could build on this land. I was ecstatic. It was going to be an amazing site. I bid for it and I paid cash $50,000. Then I went to the city of Richmond again, I said "Hey, I got it. Now I want to build something." They said, "Oh no, we are sorry. We made a mistake. You cannot build on it. It's a protected area."

Okay. It was a bad decision. I ended up selling it at a higher price at $70,000 after quite a lot of work thanks to an amazing agent. But to me, it meant that there are issues with bid4assets.com. So be extremely careful, especially if there is a home where you cannot see inside. You must factor in the risk and an additional cost for repairs. Maybe it smells, there might be mold or any other issues. So, unless you can find a way to see the entire property, I would be extremely cautious.

40)Are there 'turnkey' Airbnb investment properties?

Yes, there are different types of turnkey solutions for Airbnb investment properties.

The first is to buy a property and have a property management company take care of everything. You just give them the keys and they will manage the promotion, guests, maintenance and anything else that might come up.

The other type of turnkey solution is when a real-estate developer sells the whole or partial property and they manage everything so that you do not have to worry about the overall management.

Both are great solutions, but you need to make sure that they don't take too much money out of your asset. You have bought the property to profit for profit's sake, not to pay half of the money to someone taking care of it. You always need to check what percentage of the revenue the property management company or the developer is charging. If they take 20 to 30 per cent for everything, it is a good deal for you. If you, however, see 40 percent or more, it is a red flag and you should spend your money elsewhere.

When you are assessing whether to invest in a turnkey property, you need to make at least $1,000 per month from that property after tax. You also must ensure that your return on investment is high enough, even when you invest more money by paying the management company/developer. These properties can be great, but you need to know your numbers first.

Chapter 4: Setting yourself up for business success

If you have decided that this is the business for you, there are several things you need to know as you proceed with your business model. This chapter covers the plans you make for finding, managing, pricing and budgeting for your properties.

41) What is a good ROI for an Airbnb investment property?

Return on investment (ROI) simply means that you put some money into buying or renting a property and expect some money back. For an Airbnb investment property, I typically target properties that generate anywhere between 20 to 40 percent in returns.

I have two criteria that a property must meet for me to be interested in placing an offer:

1. **The net return on investment** (net meaning after tax) – This is essentially the money that stays in your pocket, after taxes and all the expenses, including repairs. The minimum net ROI must be at least 12 percent, otherwise, I would not buy in.

2. **The property should make at least $1,000 per month net** (also after expenses, tax, etc.)

If you wish to set the same parameters, make sure a property meets these two conditions before you even visit the place.

42) Should you avoid cities with Airbnb regulations?

You might have heard on the news that some cities regulate Airbnb rentals. You don't hear about Homeaway or Booking.com, only Airbnb. As a result, you might be asking yourself, "Is it better to avoid cities with these regulations?"

The answer is not a simple one. However, in every city where there are regulations, even in the ones that are cited as places where Airbnb is banned, there are zonings where it is perfectly okay to operate an Airbnb 365 days a year. That would not be a good headline, so the media will not tell you about those zones.

For an investor, it is about supply and demand. If you find a city with these regulations, but with zoning where it is legal to operate an Airbnb, it could be a gold mine for you as an investor. Regulations mean that there is only limited supply. If you manage to be a part of this limited supply, the demand will come.

So, should you avoid regulated cities completely? The short answer would be no. But you do need to do your homework and make sure that you are operating within a legal zoning. This is a very well-kept secret in the Airbnb property investment, as you can maximize your profit by setting your price right in a community with such limited supply.

However, finding an Airbnb friendly place is not enough; you also need to make sure that it is profitable, meaning the property is not too expensive to buy and will deliver a good return. That is why cities like New York or San Francisco are not good choices, even though there are areas where Airbnb can be operated. You would not profit from them. When you keep this advice in mind, you can set up shop in cities with Airbnb regulations.

43) Is San Diego a good market for buying Airbnb investment properties?

If you just look at the demand, San Diego might seem like a good place for Airbnb since so many people visit this city. However, just as with most big cities in the U.S., Airbnb business is heavily regulated there and is only allowed for the primary residents. If you are an investor looking to grow your business, downtown San Diego might not be the right place for you.

Additionally, in San Diego, San Francisco and New York, even if it were perfectly legal to operate an Airbnb there, you would have to pay a premium to get a property. This means a low return of investment for you, which you don't want. So, avoid the really big cities.

Heavy regulation, plus the high purchase cost of the property, would turn me off investing in a property. However, this does not mean that there are not great opportunities that are remarkably close to San Diego or any other big city. This is something that I teach in my Airbnb Cash Flow workshop. You might be able to find areas that are close to the big cities to operate an Airbnb with much better cashflow than in those cities.

44) How to find out if short-term rentals are allowed from the homeowners' association?

You need to check if your condo or apartment complex is okay for short-term rentals before investing in a property. Even if you find a great profitable place in the right zoning in the right city, the homeowners' association (HOA) of the building might still ban operating short-term rentals there. So, it is important to check with the HOA before you place a purchase offer or before you rent a place that you want to sub-lease as an Airbnb.

For this purpose, there is an important document called the Declaration of Covenants, Conditions, and Restrictions (CC&R) that you will want to seek from the HOA. This document will specify whether short-term rentals are allowed or not.

If not, it is better to stay away and focus on another property. If, however, it is allowed or it is not specified, you need to ask the HOA about this. There are ways how to add short-term rentals into the CC&R if they are not mentioned.

In any case, this document is the one you need to familiarize yourself with before placing an offer.

45) Should you have a property with or without a homeowner's association (HOA)?

My advice for investors is that their first choice should be with an HOA. This might seem counterintuitive as it involves an additional fee. However, you must keep in mind that you are paying for the certainty that the building will be well maintained. In a place without an HOA, you would be the one responsible for hiring people that can keep the environment around your property, like your yard, maintained. That could cost you more than the HOA.

Another great aspect of an HOA and its benefits are amenities. These extra are what gets your Airbnb consistent bookings. People want to stay in places with a swimming pool, a grill, a hot tub and, thanks to the HOA, access to all these services when they are part of the complex. You can even use the HOA name to market your rental to get more guests.

HOAs (and their fees) might not look like the right choice but with the right amenities in the right locations, they can be the best decision for your Airbnb property investment. They can give you peace of mind when it comes to building maintenance, which is great for your remote properties.

46) How do you manage Airbnb properties remotely?

To profit as much as possible from your Airbnb properties, sometimes you might need to venture out of your city. You might also want to do that for your own sake so you can treat yourself to a place where you like to go for a vacation. For whatever reason, you will need to manage this property from a distance.

Firstly, do not try to do it all by yourself. You need to focus your time on looking for the next property to invest in and leave booking guests to someone else. Of course, you should always stay informed about what is going on with your property but leave the responsibility of dealing with the guests to a virtual assistant, for example.

Build a good team around your property. The winning team consists of three services:

- Great cleaning services that specialize in short-term rentals. Do not hire cleaners that only come in once a month.
- A handyman for prompt repairs in case something needs fixing, including a reliable plumber for dealing swiftly with any bathroom issues.
- A good virtual assistant communicating with guests.

You might notice that I did not mention anything about getting a property manager. Please, do not hire one. You do not need them! They are just going to take 30 to 40 percent of your profit unnecessarily.

Lastly, plan ahead and duplicate your team members. Unexpected things happen, so you should always have a backup resource in case your first cleaning service or handyman quits or cannot fulfil their duties for any other reason. This is especially important when it comes to plumbers. You would not want to be left without plumbing services when the toilet breaks while guests are staying at your property.

47) Should you hire a property management company?

It does not matter whether you have one or 10 properties, having everything outsourced and taken care of while you only receive money sounds temping. But you do have to remember that you will have to give about 20 to 25 percent of your gross revenue. I have even seen commission as high as 45 percent of gross revenue going to the property management company, which is just ripping off the investor. You must be extremely careful if you are considering hiring a property management company.

I do not use their services. Instead, and I recommend all my students to do this, I have my own team as described above. It is easy to set up, you can interview them and get them on board.

Once you have established one Airbnb property in a market, you can use the "land and expand" strategy. Invest in more properties in the same area and you can use your team for all your properties there. For this you need to have a strong and reliable team. I talk more on this topic on cashflowstreet.com. Getting the right team instead of a property management company can save you a lot of money.

48) What are the financial implications for hiring a small team instead of a property management company?

Every Airbnb requires cleaning, repairs, talking to guests, and other things, which are collectively called property management. Many property management companies can provide you with these services for a cut of your revenue, typically 20-45 percent. These fees might not even include everything, you might be asked to pay additional money for cleaning supplies or other services. You need to make sure you know exactly what the fees include and because most of the time it is a substantial percentage from your revenue, it can end up costing you all of your profit.

But there is another way. I teach this in my Airbnb Cash Flow Method, but you might have already picked it up in this book as well. You can hire your team and structure its skillset so that they can take care of your property in all aspects and you can pay them a flat fee instead of the percentage of your revenue.

You need to be very disciplined when you are interviewing the people, whether it is the cleaning services or person for answering guest inquires, to make sure you hire the right team that you can count on. But do not worry, if you find out you did not hire the best person, you can always replace them after a few months if they do not perform up to your standard.

Having your team will quickly show you why it is better than hiring a property management company. On average, hosts without property management companies earn three times more. And you can reinvest the money you save faster and increase your revenue even faster.

49)Should you hire one or two cleaning teams?

When you go to a hotel, Airbnb or any place where you are going to stay through the night, the first thing you notice is if it is clean. It must be clean, and if it is not, it is frustrating for the guest as well as the host. You do not want to experience a guest calling you for a refund because that the place is not clean.

You probably have a one-night minimum stay in your place to maximize the revenue. One night means you must be very reactive with the cleaning. Sometimes you will check out and check in guests on the same day with the check-in being after a last-minute booking, but the place still needs to be cleaned properly. This puts a lot of stress on the cleaning team, especially if they are not trained for short-term rentals.

Now the question arises, should you have one or two cleaning teams to make sure that your place is always clean and ready for guests?

The answer is not so easy since it depends on the quality of the cleaning team and how much you trust them. Anything can happen; even the best cleaning team can close its business or relocate to another state. But you must make sure that you protect your business.

Generally speaking, I would say in an area where you have five properties or fewer, I would stick to one cleaning team. It should not be only one person; it should be a cleaning team and you need to make sure that they are well trained. If there are no significant issues after six months, I would keep them. If you had more than one big issue per month over the six months, I would look for a different crew.

If you have more than five properties, I would opt for two cleaning teams. Make sure that they are aware that there is another team, so they are motivated to maintain the quality. If they do not do a good job, they know they will be kicked out. And if something happens to one of the teams, the other one can take over. This will ensure that you do not have any revenue risk on your end and you maintain the quality of cleaning as high as possible.

50) How do you price your Airbnb rates?

This is probably one of the most important skills you can have to maximize your profit in this type of investment. If there are no reservations for your property for the next three months or if it is completely booked, it might indicate that there is something wrong with the prices. Either the price is too low, and every guest wants to take advantage of that, or the listing is priced too high, leaving you with no bookings.

The key is to have dynamic pricing. That means that the price changes daily based on these examples:

- whether the booking is for a weekday or a weekend;
- there is a popular event unfolding nearby;
- the reservation is made far ahead of time;
- there is only one night available between two reservations.

Airbnb has its smart pricing tool, however, there are other popular technologies designed to change the price daily. Three well-known software technologies that plug-in to your Airbnb account are Beyond Pricing, Pricelabs and Wheelhouse.

I personally use Beyond Pricing as it allows to synchronize Airbnb and VRBO listings without using property-management software. It is also really easy to set up and use. You can just log in and it automatically synchronizes your pricing. The service also shows a matrix of whether your base price (price around which the daily price fluctuates) is too high or too low and whether you should adjust it.

51) How do you make your Airbnb 'bulletproof' against risks?

Setting up a bulletproof Airbnb protection is essential for any issues with guests as you never know what might happen.

The first thing you need is insurance with three parts: personal liability, loss of revenue (in case something happens to the property that prevents you from renting it) and protection against damages (for getting reimbursement if guests damage your property). A damage deposit should be high enough to deter irresponsible behavior from renters. I recommend $300 for a studio, $500 for a one-bedroom apartment and so on.

Another great tip is to buy a Noiseaware device, which is a sensor that monitors the noise levels in the unit in real-time and can send out alerts if the sound gets too loud. It can send alert not only to you, but also to a property manager near your property so that he or she can intervene when needed.

Avoiding one-night stays can also serve as protection. You can set one night as a minimum stay to increase the number of bookings, but you also risk that people will come for one night only to party and destroy your place. You don't want that.

Having a limited liability company (LLC) is another layer of protection that can reduce your liability.

52) Should you have an LLC for your Airbnb business?

Unexpected things happen every day in life, so you always want to have the best liability protection. A limited liability company (LLC) can provide you with a layer of protection in case an incident happens in your Airbnb property, so the injured party cannot go after all your assets. Without one, a person can sue you for everything you own, including your personal savings and home.

There are, however, other ways to protect yourself without creating an LLC. The key is to have the right insurance, even if you have an LLC. There are insurance companies that specialize in short-term rentals and would cover your liability, your physical assets and the loss of revenue.

If you are open to the idea of starting an LLC, it will add the extra layer of protection and it is relatively cheap and easy to set up. It is important to set up this entity correctly and right from the beginning, so that you do not have to change the name of the entity investing in the property later.

53) How do you calculate your emergency fund for your Airbnb property?

With the economy fluctuating, some days we are in a recession, while some days are good. You will need to have an emergency fund, not just for yourself, but for your Airbnb as well. It is particularly important to have this fund, so you do not stress out when your revenue is lower than normal.

Firstly, you should list all your revenue on one side and all your expenses on the other. Naturally, for the expenses, you put the HOA, electricity bills, cable, internet and property management costs. Do not forget anything. On the other side, you have your revenue from the previous year if you are just starting, try to assess all your revenue in a normal year.

Now, expect that the expenses will stay the same, even in the recession. Your mortgage or rent, and HOA fee are not going to be reduced because of economic changes. Assume that your revenue will be divided by four. This is based on previous experience, when the average revenue during the recession went down to one-fourth of the revenue in a normal year. This is probably going to create a loss. When you look at the loss for the whole year, that should be your emergency fund.

Do not try to invest this emergency fund in buying or renting a property. Put it aside or invest it very safely. That should be your backup that you can count on in case something like recession happens.

54) What vacation rentals TV show can teach me more?

You might be wondering if there is anything on the TV about vacation rentals. Since there is a show about basically anything, there is also a show about vacation rentals.

As someone interested in this industry, you should stream a show entitled *Stay Here,* which came out recently on Netflix. I watched the whole first season in less than 48 hours and it was everything I hoped for – entertaining, fun and educational. You can see that hosts struggling in different areas – marketing, design, etc. They also cover many locations all over the United States, like Malibu, Brooklyn, even a Seattle houseboat, so each episode is different.

Many great lessons can be applied to your own Airbnb property investment, so here are my top three:

1. **Design**. A memorable interior design helps create better settings for the promotional photos in your listing. You can easily differentiate your property from others then price your property better.
2. **Experience**. Having a nice place to stay is not enough. People seek special events they can *experience* around your property, like wine tasting or unique tours. You need to provide them with opportunities for an adventure or great memory to make their stay unforgettable.
3. **It is only a TV show**. Do not forget that this is a TV entertainment. The owners might invest a lot of money in remodelling the place look special, but this is not always practical when it comes to real life. Also, the people featured on the show always already own the place, so keep that in mind that they have not put money into it recently.

I hope you will enjoy watching the show, while acknowledging that not everything they do there is a good idea for your own property-investment business.

Chapter 5: Practical tips for getting your house in order

On top of all the business decisions you need to make, there are several logistics that you need to sort out to make operations run smoothly. By setting these up early, you create a template that you can copy from one property to another.

55) Should you buy or rent the furniture?

From my experience, buy the furniture. Do so, however, for a good price, without investing too much money into it.

IKEA is a great store for Airbnb properties as they have great designs for a good price. Guests will inevitably damage the furniture; it wears out with time when it is being constantly used. That is why you do not want to spend a ton of money on easily replaceable pieces. With IKEA, the price will be roughly the same every time you need to replace items, so it is a big plus. And they also deliver, so there are fewer worries for you.

Buying and replacing furniture is part of your business investment. It is tax-deductible, so do not feel bad when you must substitute a new version.

Don't overlook the value of interior design. Just because all the furniture comes in one IKEA catalogue, it doesn't mean you should put it together in a room. Photos sell your listing, so make sure that your place is nicely decorated. If you don't have the skills yourself, hire an interior designer (you can find them on Yelp or House.com) and they will make sure that your place will attract people, even when it's full of IKEA furniture.

56) What are the top 3 mattresses for short-term rentals?

The mattress that your guests will sleep on is particularly important. If they don't sleep well, I guarantee you are going to have bad reviews. On the other hand, if you choose a good mattress and they have a great sleep, then they're going to give you an excellent review.

Make sure that you have an excellent mattress, but do not overspend money. The other day I was just looking at Bloomingdale's website and saw some mattresses that costs around $10,000. You should not spend that much money.

From my experience, I use my Airbnb from time to time and I also want to have a good quality sleep. So yes, there is a bit of a selfish aspect as well, but more importantly, you want to make sure that your guests will get an outstanding sleep.

There are a lot of choices when it comes to mattresses. I want to give you the top three mattresses that are great for investment properties and that I use again and again.

They are Casper, Zinus and Tuft & Needle. They are equally good; I have had great success with all three brands.

If you go on Amazon.com, for example, you will see that those three mattresses are not just for sale, but they can be packaged in a box. It is easy to ship them and therefore they are very affordable. The king-size mattress costs less than $800, which is great. Also, be on the lookout for coupons, especially for Casper. They do often have these. Once you have these mattresses, do not forget to also buy a mattress protector so you can safeguard your new asset and extend the lifetime of this mattress is as long as possible.

57) How do you price the cleaning fee?

The cleaning fee is a very strategic charge that doubles as a way to avoid too many one-night reservations. My advice is to set the minimum stay to one night to fill up as many blank spots between reservations in the calendar as possible. However, do not set the cleaning fee too low, otherwise, you would get too many one-night reservations and it would be difficult to fill up the calendar. This price should also be high enough to cover all your cleaning expenses – on top of the cleaning services. If your cleaning service makes you pay for cleaning products or toilet paper, or if you provide your guests with coffee, this should be included in the cleaning fee as well.

You can also determine the right cleaning fee for your listing by benchmarking the cleaning fee of other similar listings. Look at minimum of 20 similar listings, based on the same type of property in similar or the same neighborhoods, then price yourself within the top 20 percent of those listings. Don't discount too much. Make sure you cover your price and avoid too many one-night reservations.

58) Should you use a keypad lock or lockbox in your Airbnb?

A lockbox is certainly cheaper and may be easier to set up right then. It has a code just like the keypad. So why not go with the cheaper one?

When I started with my Airbnb, I put a lockbox there, so the guests could use it and I was good to go. Then I started getting some complaints from guests that did not know how to use the little number wheel on the lockbox to enter the code. It may sound easy to you as the owner. However, for guests who have made a long trip, entering a code with number wheel could be particularly difficult, especially if they have never used a lockbox before. If you have one guest out of 10 or 20 that complains and gives you a one-star review because of a lockbox, you probably should find another option.

Instead, I recommend putting in a keypad so guests can just press the buttons to enter a code. You must make it as easy as possible for them. They just need to read the welcome message with the code, press a few buttons and everything is good to go. It is the more expensive choice and you must call a locksmith to set it up, but in the long run, is going to make your life and the lives of your guests much easier.

I strongly recommend self-check-in. When guests do check-in themselves, it is best to do it with the easiest method possible. Even though you think the lockbox is easy, make it even easier. Your guests will be delighted that everything runs smoothly right from the beginning. So, keypad it is.

59) Should you have an Airbnb repair budget?

You should always be prepared with a repair budget for your Airbnb listing, whether you are renting properties and sub-leasing them, or you bought the property. There will be some issues. Trust me, I know. I have more than 20 Airbnb properties and can tell some horror stories from the sea of my students. There will have to be some repairs; it is just the cost of business. This does not mean you will just have to make some big repairs after damages, but smaller tasks such as a simple towel replacement, changing the door lock or cleaning a carpet stain. There are a lot of reasons for using a repair budget.

Like in any hospitality business, it is important that you do not get surprised by expenses to repair anything that needs to be fixed, to repair what guests break or damage. You should have a budget set aside which you can use to buy new towels, fix any plumbing issue, or fix any other issue that might arise. Those expenses are going to happen, and you should not feel bad when they do. It is just a matter of time.

60) What monthly budget should you have for Airbnb listings' repairs?

The short answer is that it depends on the size of the property. Here is the guideline: for a studio or one-bedroom put away $100 a month, for a two-bedroom $200, a three-bedroom $300, and so on. That way, you will be well covered for any repairs. I still use this guideline today and have yet to exceed this budget. All my expenses for repairs are below this budget, which is what you want.

Each time there is an expense, you can just deduct it from that budget. It is like you have already spent the money, so you will not feel as badly about it. If you have a two-bedroom, then it is $200 per month that you should put aside.

If my properties did not need as much repair, I take the money at the end of the year and use it to renovate. I have already put aside this money, so I can use it for something else, like changing the carpet at the end of two years.

Once you have these funds set aside, you can have peace of mind that your business is well funded and prepared for any of the surprises that your guests provide you with. That is one of the exciting things about Airbnb is guests. They often have surprises. You never know what they are going to break, but you will be ready.

61) Should you do a mold inspection for your Airbnb property?

When you buy a property and want to rent it on Airbnb, there are a couple of contingencies. Two of the main ones are financial contingency if you have a mortgage, and an inspection contingency, meaning you need to have an inspector go into the unit and look at everything: the plumbing, the electricity, the structure, everything. This person will make sure that everything is okay, and you are not going to have any major repairs ahead.

One of my students had a big issue because she did not have this inspection done. The financial contingency went well. She closed on the property then she started hearing from a neighbor that there is probably a mold issue. Black mold, which is extremely dangerous, can be deadly if you breathe it in. A unit with this type of contaminant cannot be rented.

If you don't catch this before a sale closes, there is a whole mess with mediation over who should pay for the renovation -- the previous owner or you. It is an extraordinarily complex issue. You can avoid all of this by adding one simple option to your general inspection, which is a mold inspection. Typically, the inspectors do not do an air sample or drill into the wall, but they do an accurate humidity assessment to assess the risks. Mold needs humidity and high temperature, so from these indicators, they can predict whether there is mold growth or not.

These are especially important tests to do. They can identify any leaks with the sensors and you can make sure that you do not have mold in the property. And if there are some leaks, you can call a second company to do the air samples and confirm whether there is mold or not. This is not going to cost you much more money, probably a couple of hundreds of dollars, but it will save you a lot of headaches and you will be able to rent it on Airbnb as soon as possible.

Chapter 6: Promoting your rentals to keep them booked up

Now that your properties are set up and you are prepared for your guests, your next focus to ensure that you have a steady stream of people staying at your properties and paying you rent. While you can just post a listing on Airbnb.com and hope for the best, you will earn far more revenue and make the most of your hard work by getting the word out in more ways. Also, there are times when a full house isn't the best option. Here are the lessons I've learned so I can share them with you.

62) Where else can you promote your listings beyond Airbnb?

Posting your listing on multiple sites will alert guests about the cozy nest you have created. You do not need to have your place on every rental site there is but selecting the few that are the best is great for maximizing revenue. I use three: Airbnb (of course), VRBO/Homeaway and Booking.com.

When using more sites to promote a listing, it is essential to have them all synchronized in a calendar to avoid double booking. iCal is a great tool that can sync all three sites. Once the place is booked through VRBO, for example, it will automatically update the availability on all other sites so that you can be sure that two guests will not show up at the same time.

When you are selecting where you will promote your listings, always look at the commission each of the sites takes. Booking.com, for instance, takes a slightly higher commission, so you should adjust the price accordingly.

There are many other sites where you can advertise, such as TripAdvisor, Flipkey or Wimdu, but it can get overwhelming to manage all the listings. Having ads on one to three sites is more than enough to keep your property well booked.

If you, however, want to have your place promoted on many sites, you might want to invest in a property-management software. That means another chunk of money out of your pocket, so you always think about whether it is worth it.

63) Do you want a 100-percent occupancy rate?

Firstly, you must ask yourself how to maximize the profitability of your property instead of how to get a 100-percent occupancy rate. Getting a full occupancy rate is easy, just price your listing at $1/night and see what happens! Will that be a good result for you? No. But you would have the 100 percent occupancy rate that you wanted.

You need to focus on how to maximize your profit or cash flow. Occupancy is just a secondary metric. You might have maximized cash flow with 85 percent or 70 percent occupancy for the market that you are in. You need to look at your pricing strategy to align with your goals. Depending on the market you are in, you need to look at different aspects of the strategy, like pricing the weekend versus the weekdays, pricing some off nights during the week, deciding whether to have discount for seven days (I usually do not recommend this but it might make sense in certain markets).

Make sure that your pricing strategy is optimized specially for the market you are in so that you can really maximize your profit and then you will see what the right occupancy for your market is.

64) What are the Top 5 Airbnb amenities?

When you are shopping around, you want to find properties with amenities that appeal to guests. Before booking, the guests will be looking at the photos of the listings, seeking these most popular luxuries. Also, Airbnb listings contain a list of all amenities so guests can easily use filters and view only the listings that come with the conveniences they desire. That is why you will want to have the most sought-after amenities. The top 5 are:

1. Hot tub – It is such a treat to enjoy a relaxing soak, especially in private.

2. Outdoor grill – Everybody loves a good barbecue. You should, however, always consider the additional cleaning costs.
3. Private pool – Although popular with guests, this is tough for the investor in terms of return on investment.
4. Washer and dryer – This additional service is very helpful for guests.
5. Stunning view.

A private pool and stunning view might not be the best in terms of ROI, as the purchasing price of the property will be so high from the beginning, limiting your initial profits. The hot tub is for your consideration, but make sure to do everything according to the homeowners' association and the CC&R.

65) How do you increase the number of your bookings during the low season?

This is a worry for a lot of investors, understandably. Following these simple steps will help you get through the low-demand seasons.

The first tip is to buy a property in a location that does not have extreme seasons in the first place. For instance, I do not usually recommend ski resorts. Unless there are a lot of tourists and attractions during the summer, the warmer months of the year will be dry for your property, lowering the overall numbers for the year.

There might also come a time where you have slower period, even if you are not somewhere with extreme seasons. At that point, you should turn your attention to two sites other than Airbnb: their competitors Booking.com and VRBO/HomeAway. On these sites, you can market to more people while synchronizing the calendars between these platforms, so you do not need to worry about complications arising from double bookings.

Another platform you should have a look at is Logify. It helps you create beautiful templates for a website for your property so that you will be searchable directly through Google, which will increase your exposure. Your site there also comes with software for managing your reservations.

Social media can also help with low seasons as well. You should be on Instagram, Twitter, Facebook and YouTube. Instagram is a great visual platform with which you can show the interior of the property in the best light, alongside its surroundings and nearby restaurants. You can post a lot of content there within reach of a dynamic community.

66) Is Booking.com a good alternative to Airbnb?

If you want to get some additional bookings, especially in the slow periods, Booking.com can provide some additional reservations. However, there are some drawbacks that you need to be aware of before posting a listing there.

Firstly, there is no damage deposit. Even if your guests demolish your property, you do not have the option to get any deposit via this platform. This means you will have to do it separately for each reservation and ask your guests for additional money for the damage deposit, which is operationally challenging. This is especially difficult for last-minute reservations.

Booking.com also has no insurance, so if anything happens in your property, you will not get any money. At most, it would pay you the commission back, which is little consolation, so you should keep this in mind.

Although Airbnb and VRBO both offer insurance, you should always have your own anyway, to minimize your liability. Even though you can get additional bookings, make sure that you are adequately covered.

67) What are the top 10 tips to improve your ranking on Airbnb?

Why is this important? Because you want to make sure that your listing is ranked as high as possible when someone searches for listings in your area. Here are the top 10 tips:

1. Make sure you have regular updates on your calendar so that Airbnb knows it is up to date.
2. Have a one-night minimum.

3. Price your Airbnb right. If it is too high, Airbnb will notice and is not going to put it high on the list.

4. Have high photo quality. Airbnb checks the quality and consistency of photos.

5. Have a well-written and complete listing.

6. Turn on the 'instant booking' setting.

7. Reply quickly to all guest inquiries. Response time is very important.

8. Put your Airbnb URL on social media. Airbnb loves free advertising and knows your listing is worth something if you put it on Instagram, Facebook or any other platform.

9. Earn five-star reviews. If your guests say that your listing is great, Airbnb is going to believe them.

10. Create a generic guidebook. Share this guidebook on Airbnb, so the company will notice that you are taking good care of your guests.

All these tips are easy to implement and will pay off when you earn the trust of more guests with a higher ranking.

68) Can you change an Airbnb review after you write it?

As you know, on Airbnb you can review your guests and they can review you. It is not always a great experience. You will get surprised sometimes when your guests who seemed genuinely nice and kind will then give you a bad review. At other times, hard-to-please guests that were very picky will leave a great rating.

You may have experiences with guests that do not say anything at first. Everything seems okay, with no communication with you then they drop a bombshell. That happens as well.

I am incredibly grateful to be a Super Host, but it takes a lot of work. Many of you know that getting more than 4.8 out of five is difficult. But you still cannot please all your guests. Sometimes you want to make sure you do not try to review too quickly.

Let's say a guest checked out and everything seemed well. The minute they left, you write a review that this was a wonderful guest and everything went well. You submit it to Airbnb but then you get the feedback from your cleaning team that says, "This guest left the place in a mess. They did not respect the house rules." The extra hours and work of cleaning cost you extra, so this person was not a good guest.

But you have already submitted the review to Airbnb. Can you change it? If you have submitted the review but the guest has not yet done so, you can still edit and change it. The review needs to be accurate to help future hosts know each renter is a good guest or if they rather should avoid them.

To do so, you need to go on airbnb.com, go to your profile, then click on reviews. Then you select "Reviews by You." Find the review that you would like to edit, write an accurate description, click submit and that is it.

69) What are the five most valuable tips for great Airbnb photos?

I am going to share with you five tips to make the most of your listing. Only one of these tips could double the revenue you have on your listing if you do it well.

You must pay attention to the photos. They convey more than 90 percent of the value of your Airbnb. Why? Because people do not visit your Airbnb before their stay. They look at the photos and that is how they decide where to rent. Only some people are going to read the description in detail, but all of them will look at the photos. I wish more people would read the description, but they will base their decision on the photos, the amenities they chose with the filter, and whether they have the whole place or just the room. Their decision consists of these three things.

That is why good photos are crucial. And these tips can help you get them:

1. **Get a professional to take your photos.** I know iPhones have a gazillion cameras on them nowadays, but you are not going to do as well as a professional photographer. Do not do it yourself. Hire a photographer to take beautiful photos. If you do not know how to find a

photographer, just check house.com or yelp.com and look at people that specialize in real estate photographs.

2. **Describe what is on the photo**. Do not just post the photos; the captions are important as well. Airbnb has changed the size and location of photos and captions so that captions are now more visible. Make sure that you label the exact photo with what room it is, along with other details. It may be obvious for you, but it is not for your guests. Also, be creative with the captions. If you do not have the right words in your imagination, put a quote from your previous guests that relate to the photo. If they said, "I love the view from this window" or "These were the most comfortable sheets to sleep in," add it in the caption of the photo.

3. **Screenshot good reviews** and insert them in the pictures. If you have many good reviews, put them right under the nose of your future guests. It is more likely they will see these reviews if you present the good ones like a photo. Before you know it, more prospective guests will want to come if that many people enjoyed their previous stays.

4. **Add a picture of the floorplan of your listing**. There are different services online where you can set the dimensions, and you can present a two-dimensional floor plan of the place. This will help guests imagine how the

condo or house looks even before they arrive, so they can pre-plan accommodation.

5. **Show the neighborhood**. Do not just play up the value of your place and make it sound like a great place to visit. Alongside your best photos, add photos of your neighborhood. They can come from Google, but make sure that you outline the experience they can have outside of your home. It could be the forest right around the corner, the beach or a nice restaurant or a coffee shop. This makes your listing very cozy, comfortable and unique *and* it will help you differentiate your place from your competitors.

70) How do you become a Super Host?

That is the million-dollar question! Everybody wants to be a Super Host. If you already have a property listed on this platform, you might know that it is not so easy to become one. You must know what you are doing.

Timely answers are essential in becoming a Super Host. You must answer your guests very quickly, plus find an answer to all their questions before and during their stay. If you do not have the time, hire a virtual assistant that will answer any question your guests might have.

You also must make sure that your property is amazingly comfortable, meaning with great interior design that not only looks good on the photos but feels good in real life. The interior must make your guests feel great from the moment they open the door. If you do not know how to create such space, hire a professional interior designer that will help you create this magical environment.

Set up your place with things that are popular and that people like. A Nespresso machine is great and easy to use. As a bonus, you can buy the coffee pods anywhere. Guests will appreciate it much more than putting a huge complicated Keurig coffee maker in the kitchen. You can see that even high-end hotels specifically have Nespresso machines for guests because they are so popular. Put brand new bottles of water in the fridge, not the ones you refill. Put nuts or other small bites in cute packaging on the table. It is not going to cost you a lot of money, but it will be a nice touch. You can also leave a small bottle of champagne or a bottle of wine in a fridge. Do not spend a lot of money but also do not buy the cheap stuff. Make sure that you treat your guests well. They will notice and Airbnb will too.

71) Can you book hotels on Airbnb?

You can book boutique hotels through Airbnb; this is the one exception for hotels there is. However, as Airbnb is continuously expanding and penetrating new markets, it starts to focus on the highly profitable hotel market as well.

Airbnb has launched Airbnb Plus which is a list of Airbnb properties that are not hotels but look and feel like a hotel with hotel-like quality. The listings must pass a 100-point quality checklist, so they are pretty much standardized in terms of shampoo brand or the number of towels.

They have also bought the company HotelTonight which specializes in last-minute hotel reservations. Airbnb recognizes that even though the home-sharing market is large, the traditional accommodation market is even larger. People want to stay in a hotel, and this is not going to change.

And I do not think that Airbnb is going to stop here. Recently, Airbnb hired the aviation industry pioneer Fred Reid as the global head of transportation, which is signaling a move towards handling airline flights.

72) Where else can you list your property and get more bookings?

What are the main competitors or where should you list your property beside Airbnb to get more bookings? Although Airbnb is massively dominating the market with more than seven million listings, there are times when you have some vacancies, when you need to increase the number of bookings.

I remember when this happened to my property in Canada about four years ago. I decided to look at the competitors, and there were several because it is a growing market.

So here are some alternatives. I am sure you have never heard of some of them but try to assess each of them and see which one is a better fit for you. In the end, I will let you know which one is my best alternative to Airbnb.

The competitors are Tripping.com, HomeToGo, Flipkey, HomeAway/VRBO, House Trip, VacayHero and Wimdu. Then there is also Booking.com. You may have seen its advertising. The two main alternatives to Airbnb that you may consider are Booking.com and HomeAway/VRBO.

I will focus on VRBO and not Booking.com for the simple reason that I do not think Booking.com is safe for hosts. With them, you would not have any security deposit and the system of vetting guests is not particularly good. So, Airbnb and VRBO are much safer for your property's sanctity. You can set a security deposit, which limits the number of damage-related issues.

I consider VRBO to be the competitor where you post your listings alongside Airbnb. It is also easy to synchronize the calendars on those sites, so you avoid double bookings and can maximize the number of bookings.

Chapter 7: Welcoming and managing your guests

You have reached that magical moment where your first guests arrive to enjoy the property you have so lovingly created for them. It is a landmark moment for you. To make them feel welcome and comfortable, there are some extra steps you can take to go beyond the typical Airbnb experience. However, some visits don't go as smoothly as others so you will want to brace yourself for some bad behaviours and decide ahead of time how you want to handle them.

73) What if a guest asks 50 questions before checking-in?

If you are Airbnb or VRBO host already, I am sure can relate to this. I once hosted this guest who pretty much asked me to organize his honeymoon in the area a month before his stay. He asked me to set up a wine-tasting tour, hot-air balloon tour, restaurant reservations, and so on. I found it quite odd, to be honest.

Next, the guest asked a lot of detailed questions, for instance, for the exact brand of the coffee machine and the exact distance from point A to point B. As soon as my team or I answered his questions, a million other questions came flooding in.

If you read the book from Perry Marshall *The 80/20 rule*, you know that some guests are just not good for your business. They are going to drain so much of your time, not just 80 percent. If you have such guests that are asking more and more, you must set clear expectations. Explain exactly what services you do offer and what they should and should not expect from you.

In my case with this high-maintenance guest, I was not a honeymoon planner. I was there to provide him with the best experience with my Airbnb property, but scheduling is not a service I provide. We do give recommendations and he is welcome to ask for those.

But if you do have a guest who is still asking too much from you, even after you have explained everything, you can say that you do not think your listing is the right one for him. You can kindly explain that if he needs other services, maybe a different listing would suit him better. Ask him to start a cancellation process from his side so that your Airbnb is not hit with a fine. Sometimes, it is best not to be greedy and want to have every guest. If you see this type of behavior, make sure you take action early on.

74) What do you do if a guest damages your Airbnb property?

First things first, serious damage occurs very rarely. You might hear about them on TV from time to time, but they are not the norm, so you should not worry.

Smaller damage happens sometimes and that is completely normal in the hospitality business as well as in the rental business, even with long-term rentals.

Here are my 3 tips on how to handle these situations:

1. **Security deposit** – Make sure you have one. I suggest putting a flat rate, for example, of $200. A deposit that is too high might scare guests away, but you also do not want to set it too low because people might be negligent.

2. **Absorb damages lower than $100** – Do not sweat about any damages lower than $100, even if it was the fault of the guest. This is the cost of business. Demanding money for every broken glass might get you some unfavorable reviews and that will cost much more than the damage itself.

3. **Submit a payment request for damages higher than $100** – Do this before the next guest checks in, otherwise, Airbnb is not going to help. Make sure that you or your team take plenty of photos to prove the damage, in case the guest does not want to pay.

Also, set aside a budget for the damages so that you can deal with them as soon as possible. Follow these tips and you will be perfectly fine in such situations.

75) How can you guests from hosting parties in your Airbnb?

This is one of the scariest things for Airbnb hosts. You expect two guests that booked your place for a getaway but then hundreds of people show up and trash the place. We see it a lot in the news. The media likes to talk about the stories where a specific house was trashed, or where too many people damaged the property. The first thing to remember is that this is just a tiny percentage of all Airbnb properties rented all over the world.

With my 20-plus properties, this has happened once. It was a pretty bad experience, to be honest, but I got lucky with only $1,000 in damages. It was more a disturbance for the neighbors than anything else. When it happened, only one person booked the apartment. It is not a big apartment, with only around 500 square feet, and 30 people came to celebrate his birthday. Imagine 30 people in such a tiny space. It was a learning experience for me to make sure that this does not happen again. It made me think about what type of technology I can put into the apartment to avoid this.

If your home or your apartment is in a location where there could be parties, for example, in Las Vegas or Miami beach, your property is going to be more prone to these gatherings. You can set up two specific devices to help you monitor your property and act if needed. The first device is a ring doorbell. It has a video camera that sends the video to your phone so you can watch what happens outside of your property. When your guests arrive, you can see the number of people that show up. If there are too many people coming in, you can take action and have your manager on-site call the guests and explain to them that this is not going to happen.

The second option is a device called Noiseaware. It records the average level of noise inside your property. If there is a party and the music is too loud this device is going to spike up and alert you. You cannot, of course, listen to conversations, which would be illegal, but you would know the actual average level of sound and get notifications on your phone. Again, if something is wrong, you can have your property manager visit the site.

The third thing I suggest is not a device. If you are very worried that your guests may have parties, you should do an in-person check-in with your property manager that would give the key personally to your guests. He would see how many people are there and you would have a witness to how many people are coming. Some people only select Airbnb properties with self-check-in so that it is easier for them to set up a party and not be seen. So, if you are very worried you can have an in-person check-in process.

76) Should you ask a guest to pay for soiled towels?

Should you ask a guest to reimburse something that is broken or damaged in your Airbnb? You must be incredibly careful about these requests because that may cost you more than the money you are trying to get. I use a rule of thumb that if there is damage that is less than $100, I will just let it be.

It is the cost of business. I will give you a specific example with towels. A lot of guests would mistreat those nice white towels that you purchase with your own money. And if you go on Airbnb for resolutions and you ask for $55 back from your guests, they are not going to be happy, even though it is their fault. What is going to happen is they are going to give you an unbelievably bad review which will cost you much more than $55.

So, make sure that you do not try to get every penny back for the things that your guests broke, even if they were your favorite items that you had in your apartment. Damaged linens or towels are just the cost of business. You need to have a budget on the side to make sure that you can cover those small damages and don't sweat it. If it's less than $100, just let it be so you do not have to pay for it with a bad review.

77) Should you buy a new dish sponge for each new guest?

I don't know about you, but when I go to a hotel or an Airbnb, probably the most important thing is that you feel that you are the very first guest ever coming into the space.

You do not want to see hair. You do not want to see stains or a dirty kitchen. And what I think is particularly important in the kitchen is the dish sponge. It can be full of bacteria if it has been used before. This may sound like a detail, but one of the most important things that are going to make a great impression on your guests is to have a brand-new sponge inside the plastic packaging. I insist on this.

Do not just go buy a pack of 40 sponges at Costco and think that it does not matter that it is open for guest to pull out a new one. No. Make sure that it is inside the plastic packaging when you leave it there. They are going to feel like it is a free sponge just for them. But it is not a free one and is included in the price of the listing.

But this "detail" is going to make a good impression on the guests and can bring you more five-star reviews for the cleanliness of your apartment. So, pay attention to this detail, make sure you train your cleaning team to bring a new sponge every time so all the guests can feel like they are the inaugural ones.

78) Should you recommend restaurants to your guests?

In the past, when you went to a hotel, typically you had a room and that was pretty much it. Then if you went to a four-star hotel, you would talk to a concierge to get some tips on where to go. You may have or may not have liked the recommendations, but historically this was pretty much the only way you could get any information about places to go in your vacation city.

Then along came the internet. It gives you thousands of choices, confusing and overwhelming people with so many options. There are all these four- or five-star restaurants everywhere according to the internet. How should guests know which place is the best?

This is where your expertise comes into play. Guests will value genuine feedback from a person that has lived in the neighborhood and recommends favorite restaurants. You should give them at least five suggestions. But do not just give the name of the restaurant. Tell them what you like from the menu. Tell them which dish is your favorite. You should also put this in the welcome message as well. Have a section about the restaurant in your guidebook. Give them details on what is good about this restaurant. Do not just tell them, "Go to Bob's pizza." Tell them what your favorite pizza is and what drinks you like to order.

You should also do this for activities, not just restaurants. This is one of the things your guests are going to value highly. Make them feel like locals right away. They are probably going to mention it in their reviews as well.

People follow the recommendation of the welcoming message often and that leads to other business ideas. You should probably get something back from those restaurants. If you want to take it one step further, you can actually go to those restaurants, get some coupons and maybe get some free pizza or free meals from a gift card from the restaurant for you.

But most importantly, make sure your guests have the best experience possible at your place by giving them your favorite experiences all around. You will see it pay off in their reviews.

79) Should you give welcome gifts to your guests?

When you go to an Airbnb, it is all about the personal touch. Hotels now sometimes try to do it as well. You may have seen chocolates in your hotel room or, if you stay in a nice hotel, you may find some fruit or even a bottle of champagne waiting for you in your room. But this is quite rare in hotels overall, except for that very tiny chocolate that you miss on the pillow, then discover it stuck to the sheets in the morning.

In Airbnb, you often use the self-check-in and you may never even meet your guests. However, you still want to personalize your property for your guests as much as possible. You can make their experience enjoyable without being present with a nice welcoming gift. That is always a nice touch. Something that you can personalize.

Now, some gifts are certainly better than others, but you do not need to go overboard. I would not spend more than $10 to $15 for gifts but make sure that it is something that they will appreciate. For example, I used to leave a great bottle of wine for the guests. It was a wine country, so usually, the guests would have a wine-tasting activity planned already, then come to the place drunk and see another bottle on the table. They would usually share the bottle back with me in one form or another. So wine was not going over very well.

I changed the gift to some nuts and a nice bottle of water. They usually come back thirsty and what is nicer than a chilled bottle of quality sparkling water? Of course, you can leave some nice coffee pots for the coffee machine.

It is not just about the gift itself; it must look good as well. Have it packaged in special little gift bags. You can buy tons of them on Amazon. Put a couple of goodies in the bags. They do not have to cost much but people will feel like you have spent some extra money on them. But guess what? They paid for it. They paid premium for the goodies that will ultimately lift their rating.

This plays on the reciprocity principle. You give them something, they give you something back. And if there is something they are not pleased with; they tend to complain less if you have already given them a nice personalized welcoming gift. It goes a long way. You are still going to have some complaining guests from time to time. From my experience, it happens about once in 20 guests. But the gifts certainly limit this number of unhappy guests because they give a particularly good first impression.

80) What should you do if a guest smoked in your listing?

Should you bill your guests if they smoked in your place even though it is forbidden? As you know, you can set house rules for your listings. These are golden rules for any Airbnb hosts because it is how you get respect. You give your place to the guests, whether it's a room in your home or an investment property, and they must follow the rules you set. These could be rules like no parties, no smoking or no pets. Those are the typical ones that you often see on an Airbnb. But even though these are the rules, not everyone is going to follow them.

From time to time, your guests may decide that they want to smoke. It can be cigarettes; it can also be something else. After the guests leave, your cleaning team comes to your property and they tell you that there is distinct cannabis smell everywhere. But you have second guests coming in four hours. What should you do?

Firstly, do not try to contact the guests that caused this. Even though they broke the rules, there is nothing you can do and you will not get money from them. Focus on preparing the place for the next guests. Use air fresheners, open the windows and clean everything properly to get the smell away. Afterward, contact Airbnb and tell them exactly what happened. Your goal isn't to get money for the damage, but so that they know about this incident in case the next guests have any problems related to the previous guests' behaviors.

Getting money back for this kind of issue would be ridiculously hard, since resolving issues on Airbnb is very image-centric. You cannot take a photo of the smell. Broken windows or dirty towels are easy to prove, but it is exceedingly difficult with a smell. You should still inform Airbnb about this issue even though you will not get any compensation.

You can also stress in your welcome message that the listing is non-smoking. You can go one step further and place a sign inside the unit that says that it is a no-smoking area. If someone wants to smoke, they will but this may help you stop most people from lighting a cigarette.

81) What are the eight plants that Airbnb guests cannot kill?

I have set up a lot of Airbnbs and when I do, I try to make sure that there are some greens there before I take the photos to promote the property on Airbnb. Of course, if you can put plastic plants in the photos, you will not see the difference, but plastic is not very eco-friendly. If you opt for a live plant, it will not only make the place livelier for the guests, but they will feel that you care about the place. They will feel that this personal touch makes this a place to live and not just a setting from an interior decoration magazine. So, let's jump straight into the nine plants.

The first one is quite easy to remember. It is called **a ZZ plant**. The Zamioculcas zamiifolia plant is indestructible, you just cannot kill it. You can try it. Also known as a Zanzibar gem, it is native to East Africa, but it can survive in low light, even in no light at all. So, the ZZ plant is quite easy to manage.

The next one is called **a snake plant.** It is robust and it grows very tall, so it is great to fill up narrow spaces. It is also an excellent air-purifying plant.

The next one I want to mention is **a monstera deliciosa**. Also known as a Swiss Cheese plant, it looks really nice. You can look up the pictures of it on Google.

Then there is a **neon pothos**. It is a genuinely nice plant that also extremely hard to kill. I mean, if you try hard, I am sure you can kill, but if you do not run it over and water it from time to time, it will be fine.

One of my favorite plants for photos is the **rubber plant**. It can grow up to be more than 100 feet tall in native Asia, but obviously, it does not grow that high in indirect light inside. If you water it once a week, it will be a great air cleaner that removes toxins from the air. It is also so beautiful, and you can even buy it on Amazon.

The **yucca** or majesty palm tree is a quite common plant. You have probably seen it everywhere in Home Depot.

The **parlor palm** is very solid and durable plant. It is a member of the palm family.

The last recommendation is an **aloe vera**. I am sure you have heard about it or have eaten it. It is beautiful and extremely hard to kill. And if it dies, you can eat it. It is a nice addition to the plant collection within your property.

As you can see, there are lots of choices for plants that your guests will love. My favorite one is the rubber plant but go with your taste. See which ones you like with the understanding that your guests just cannot kill these variations.

Chapter 8: Ramping up your return on investment

So far, the focus has been on getting you established and making great first impressions. Now, it's time to take things to the next level and accelerate your plans towards your next set of goals. Perhaps you want to save up to buy another property. Maybe you want to treat yourself after working so hard to generate revenue from your first or second property. Whatever you have planned for your money, there are several ways to go from good revenue to great. If you're ready to hit the gas, let's jump right in.

82) How fast can you profit from an Airbnb property?

The answer depends on a few factors. Firstly, you need to make sure that you chose a profitable property. Not only profitable, but greatly profitable.

Assuming you find a property with that potential, be prepared to accept that you are not going to see profit from the moment you post your first listing. You need to market your property, get people to know it before it can fulfil its investment potential, even if you have the best place with the best promotional photos.

Airbnb is also going to be cautious with promoting your property in the search from the beginning. They, understandably, promote properties with a proven record of profitability and with a high number of bookings more than properties that have yet to earn that trust.

Typically, it takes around one to two months to get the profit your property deserves, when you market it correctly. Do not get discouraged if you do not see the money you anticipated within the first weeks. I have seen many people generate a lot of profit, even in the first two months. After the initial months, the profit grew even higher. Be patient as it will take time for your property to get recognized and reach its full potential.

83) What are three tips to scale your Airbnb empire?

One of the biggest mistakes I see with Airbnb hosts and investors is that they try to do everything themselves. They clean themselves; they talk to the guests; they manage any escalations with Airbnb and they just do not have the time to grow their business. They are limited to only up to five properties because they could not do everything themselves if they had more.

If you want to scale your operation massively, you need to outsource these responsibilities and follow these three tips:

1. **Automate emails** that repeat for each guest (e.g., check-in and check-out procedures) – I recommend smartbnb.io. It is easy to use and worth the money for the time that you save.

2. Hire a **virtual assistant** to manage emails that cannot be automated. Hire a freelancer (through Upwork for example) to send and answer any email that cannot be automated. Look at Upwork, post a job and evaluate the candidates. Once you set up a contract, just add them as a co-host to your properties and let them deal with the guests.

3. Use the **"land and expand" strategy** – Instead of buying 10 properties in 10 different cities, try to focus on one location and get 10 properties there before you move to another area. This way, you can use the same cleaning team, plumber and handyman for all your properties and run your operation much more efficiently.

84) Why should you focus on a financial metric other than your Airbnb revenue?

I interact with a lot of Airbnb hosts because they are my students. They seem to measure their success by the revenue they make. But it is not that important.

I do not care about my revenue. As with any investor, whether Airbnb, long-term lease or any other type of investment, what matters most to me is the cash flow. That means what you truly generate and what really stays in your pocket at the end of the month. It is crucial to assess vacation rentals based on the cash flow they generate monthly. There is a specific way to calculate this metric for properties. You must measure the success of your properties based on the cash flow you generate and the amount of money needed to create this cash flow.

To give you an example, you could be making $5,000 per night in a villa and think it is great. After all, $5,000 a night is a lot of money. But if you look at your expenses, it may cost you $8,000 just to operate the villa every day. Suddenly you are losing money. That is why looking at the cash flow rather than revenue is important.

Generating good cash flow requires some knowledge to assess the properties and to measure it correctly. Once you learn it, you can use it again and again to generate a lot of money.

85) What ROI can you expect from a vacation rental?

ROI stands for return on investment. You put money in a real estate asset, and you get some money back at the end of the month or the end of the year. You can easily calculate this number.

I remember when I first started buying Airbnb investment properties. I did not know what to expect because it was a new type of real estate asset for me and I was quite new in the industry. I did not evaluate how much money I would need.

There is, of course, the down payment, but there are also some closing costs, that could be quite unique for each property. If you finance it as a vacation rental, it is different than as with a primary residence for example.

You add everything up, including the setup costs of the property. Depending on whether it's a studio, one-bedroom, two-bedroom apartment, or home, you're going to have different expenses, such as a sofa, TV, and other furnishings, to make your property look and feel good.

With my first property, I tried to make it look good, but on top of that, I decided to renovate it. I went on this spending spree to have a nice interior. When it was time to calculate the ROI, it was seven percent, which is not particularly good for Airbnb. Some investors may say, "Yeah, that's fantastic. I want to buy 20 of those." However, in the Airbnb world, it is not good.

I found this out only later by buying properties that are already renovated. I just hate doing renovations. You must spend money after closing, stress about the renovation going smoothly and delay renting it out during that time. Now I look at properties that do not need renovation and I am also getting much better in cost-effectively furnishing them.

Also, more importantly, you need to buy properties in highly profitable locations. If you buy a place that is in a bad location, no matter how pretty you are going to make it look on the photos on your Airbnb listing, no one will want to go there because it is just not in the right spot for the tourists or business travelers.

So, let's answer our question what return on investment to expect with an actual number. The typical ROI is between 20 to 40 percent when you know exactly where and how to invest for vacation rental.

We know that the vacation rentals generate overall three times more profit than a traditional long-term real estate investment. But you need to know exactly what to do, including watching costs and focusing on the right numbers.

86) How do you price my Airbnb to maximize revenue?

This is the number one thing to learn because you do not want to leave money on the table. You must be competitive, especially in the low seasons, when you set the price for your property right, getting more guests coming to your place and maximizing your revenue. You have several choices on how to do it.

Firstly, you can do nothing. Just set a flat price for the week and a flat price for the weekend (that is a bit higher). This is a bad strategy but is still used quite often by hosts on Airbnb because it is simple. But they are missing out on so much money this way.

The second option is to use pricing tools such as Beyond Pricing, Pricelabs, Wheelhouse pricing, and so on. These tools are very analytical, but it takes hours to optimize the price: changing it up and down, trying to figure out the base price and forcing the price on the weekend so it is not too low. This can get very time consuming and you still do not have the certainty that you are getting every dollar possible from your property.

The third option is a method I developed because I did not see the right tool to get the highest revenue possible anywhere. It is called Cash Flow Cal and it is based on different occupancy rates with different timelines to see in which direction you need to change your price to be competitive. It is a simple pricing tool and you can come back to it every week or every month to change the price to have the biggest revenue possible. You can find it on cashflowcal.com.

87) Is a 100 percent occupancy rate good or bad for your Airbnb listing?

A lot of people will ask me "Hey, what is your occupancy rate?" or say "You don't have a 100 percent occupancy rate? Maybe that's bad." People have this is kind of obsession with rates, thinking it should be as high as possible, right? To perform well, you must have 100 percent occupancy, right? It must be better than if you had a 70 percent occupancy rate.

This is what I was thinking when I first started as well. But then I found out that this approach is so wrong. At the end of the day, your bank account is not going to show the occupancy rate you had in percentage. The last time I checked, it shows a dollar amount. What is important is how much money you make.

You need to maximize your revenue based on the profitability of your Airbnb. If you look at the yearly occupancy, more often than not, it should not be a 100 percent. I am sure that if I price my Airbnb at $1 per night, I am going to have 100 percent occupancy, but I am going to make $30 per month. That is pretty bad in my book.

You need to make sure that you optimize your pricing so that you maximize the revenue, not occupancy. So, when people tell me "Hey, I have full occupancy of the apartment on Airbnb for the next five months. This is wonderful." Well, this is bad. Your price is too cheap. You are leaving money on the table.

You should always look at how to optimize your revenue and your occupancy. There are different tools based on occupancy to help you do that. One of them is Cash Flow Cal. Pricing and optimizing the number of dollars you get are an especially important part of managing your Airbnb property.

88) What are the two critical things in your Airbnb listings that really need your attention?

When you look at the website where you are filling out information about your listing, there are several boxes there, from the title, to amenities, accessibility and photos. You have literally hundreds of things that you can tweak and customize. If you have a lot of time, you can fill out everything. Add a ton of information. But always keep your guests in mind.

So, what are the two most important things your guests are going to look at besides the price? The photos and the reviews.

You have read this in this book before, you must have professional photos for your listing. Do not just choose one photographer unless you have a great experience with him already. Choose three. You might think that this will be a lot of money just for photos, but in the long run, it is going to pay off. If you have more properties in the area, you can only choose the best one to have great photos. The upfront cost for the photographers makes a huge difference. These images are what make the guests choose you over somebody else. This is the most important thing on your listing.

Remarkably close in terms of importance are the reviews from your guests. You are going to have great reviews, good reviews, and yes, even some bad ones. Even if you try your hardest, you just cannot please some guests. But what you can do is answer the reviews. If you can reply to 100 percent of the reviews, even the good ones, then great. It shows that you are a great host that cares about your guests. You are responsive and pay attention, taking feedback seriously.

You can answer a good review with a simple "Thank you. We appreciate that you stayed with us and look forward to hosting you again." If it is a bad review, always sleep on it. After 24 hours, you need to respond without emotion but go straight to the facts. Also, always use the sandwich method, meaning say something positive, then put the constructive feedback for the guest then finish positively again. You can say, "Thank you very much for staying in our place, it was a pleasure to host you." That is a positive beginning you can use even if the guest left extremely negative feedback. Then share the constructive feedback you want them to know, such as "I wish you would have said something during your stay. We did not hear from you, so we assumed everything was okay. I am surprised to hear that you did not find the bedding as comfortable as you wanted." Then finish with something positive, like "We really hope to make your stay even better next time and look forward to hosting you again." That would be a great public review.

If you pay attention to these two things, your Airbnb ranking is going to go up and you will get much more revenue.

89) Can you use the Airbnb Cash Flow Method to invest in Airbnb properties overseas?

My Airbnb Cash Flow Method is applicable in any country that has either tourists or business travelers, or both. The same rules for identifying the right property can be applied to any place in the world that fulfills this condition.

However, I always advise selecting a property in a place where you can arrive via a direct flight within fewer than six hours. Even though you will not be running it all on your own, for your peace of mind, it is better to choose places that are closer to you so you can get there if an unexpected situation arises. Also, choose a place where you can speak the language, for the same reason.

Personally, I would love to own a property in Italy, but I do not speak Italian. If I needed to arrange something with a constructor or a neighbor, it would be challenging. Since I am living in San Francisco, it would also be too far for me to manage. But I do have students that speak the language and are phenomenally successful with their properties there.

Generally, it depends on your situation geographically (you should be able to get there with a direct flight in fewer than six hours) and on your language skills.

90)Should you invest $100,000 in upgrading your current Airbnb or buy a new Airbnb property?

When you are deciding whether to upgrade what you have or invest in a new property, first you have to look at the incremental cash flow that the upgrade would bring you. How much more would you profit each month with the upgrade compared to the property without the upgrade? How do you do that? Look at the comparable listings that already have the upgrades you are thinking of adding. That will give you a pretty good idea of how much more you could get. Also, look at the cash on cash return for that upgrade. This can be calculated by taking the incremental cash flow divided by the total cash spent on this upgrade.

Once you have these two metrics, find out the cash flow and cash on cash also for the new property you would want to buy and rent through Airbnb. Compare the numbers you would get from upgrading your property to the numbers you would get from investing in the new property. You will see which choice would be more profitable for you, even though you would be spending the same amount of money. Then you have your answer!

91) What is Airbnb Plus?

Airbnb Plus means hotel-like listings. Airbnb tries hard to get into the hotel market and hotels try to get into the Airbnb market, so there is this conversion. As of February 2020, there are more than 26,000 Plus listings on the site available in 41 cities worldwide. This is the new selection of the highest quality homes that are unique, with great reviews and attention to detail.

To get on the Airbnb Plus, someone from Airbnb must visit you and evaluate the quality of your home with a 100-point inspection checklist to ensure that everything is up to the Plus standard. And what is the benefit? Very likely you will have a premium listing and you will get more bookings. The exact percentage of revenue increase is not known, but you will be promoted as a high-end listing, so you can expect more bookings.

There are two ways how to get on the list. Firstly, Airbnb Plus can contact you directly, which happened to a couple of my properties. Secondly, you can request for Airbnb to consider you for an inspection visit (Airbnb.com/plus/host) and see if you get selected.

92) What are the top 3 smart products for your Airbnb?

Smart products can not only make the stay more comfortable for your guests but can help you run your operation smoothly.

The first one I would recommend investing in is the ring doorbell (which you can learn more about on the next page). With this gadget, you can have a camera right in front of your property, and, when your guests ring it goes straight to your phone so you can talk to them right away. This tool can help you verify whether only the announced guests are coming and serve as a quality assurance to check how long cleaning service employees were at your place. It is a must for monitoring your Airbnb.

A thermostat is the second smart tool I always recommend as it will save you a lot of money. Guests usually do not care whether the heat or the AC is on the whole day while they are out and about. With the smart thermostat, you can control the temperature and check it on your phone remotely through Wi-Fi.

The third one is a smart lock, with which you can see exactly when guests check in and out. Personally, I use Schlage smart locks which allow me to give guests a simple code to use. You can also connect it to Wi-Fi and check when guests check-in/out and whether they follow the rules.

93) How can you easily increase my Airbnb revenue by 10 to 50 percent with one easy-to-use tool?

How can the pricing tool called Cash Flow Cal help your Airbnb property increase revenue by 10 to 50 percent? This tool was built to maximize the revenue that each Airbnb host can generate. It applies to all cities worldwide, not just in the US.

As an engineer, I developed it myself because I felt that my own set of properties could perform better. I wanted better guidance in terms of what pricing should I have. How much should I increase or decrease the pricing in the high season and the low season?

Every day, this tool measures the health of your property based on the occupancy rates in the next 30, 60 and 90 days. Once the algorithm measures these factors, it can provide you with simple recommendations on how you should adapt your pricing. Should they remain the same? Should you increase it by $20 by $40 or decrease by $20 or $40 to maximize the revenue on your property?

You can work directly with the Airbnb pricing tool or use other pricing tools like Beyond Pricing, Pricelabs or Wheelhouse pricing but they do not give you this base price recommendation. You will probably spend hours trying to figure out the base price yourself.

That is what this tool is about. It is amazingly simple. I am just so addicted to it and use it every single day just to monitor the health of my properties. And I am sure you will see the same effect on your property. Check it out at https://www.cashflowstreet.com/home.

94) How can you use 'ring doorbell' monitoring to increase your Airbnb revenue by 10 percent?

As you know, when guests are booking a stay, they must enter the right number of guests that will be arriving at your place. Usually, I keep the price the same for one or two guests but if there are three or more coming, this should be reflected on the price. I charge $40 per night for each additional guest above the initial two people.

However, sometimes guests intentionally or unintentionally do not provide the correct number of guests and indicate that fewer people would be coming than there are in reality. This allows them to avoid paying extra fees for additional guests. You can remind them in a message to check if they do have the correct number of guests indicated. Tell them you need to prepare the towels and linens for everyone and that you also need specific numbers for insurance purposes. Some guests might want to "trick the system" and pay as little as possible, so they will not update the number of guests.

For these situations, it is beneficial to have a ring doorbell pro, which can be hardwired in front of your property. This way, you will be able to see the surroundings right at the front door, monitor if the correct number of guests checked in and take action in case there are any issues.

Do not monitor the property yourself as it would take you a lot of time. Hire a freelancer (through Upwork or similar platforms) that you will add to the monitoring system. This person can monitor your property during the check-in times and contact Airbnb on your behalf in case any updates to the number of guests are needed.

95) What are two tips to maximize your Airbnb tax return?

Doing your tax return the right way can save you thousands of dollars. These are my two main tips:

1. **Do not do it alone** – There are changes implemented to tax laws every year, so you want to make sure that you have the best certified professional accountant (CPA) that will guide you through the process. You should find a CPA that has experience with short-term rentals. It may sound obvious, but as with banks, some CPAs have never done tax return for short-term rentals and some that are experts in this.

2. **Make sure that you have all your deductions** – Many people leave too much money to the IRS just because they do not have all the expenses classified. They do not add all their expenses to their tax return as deductions. But do not add anything unnecessary either. Follow the IRS guidelines. According to these, the expense needs to be both necessary and ordinary. Do not forget to add your travel expenses that were related to your Airbnb business. But these too must fulfill the two criteria for expenses. First-class flight tickets to your Airbnb for a family vacation cannot be deducted. Car travel expenses when you went to do basic repairs on the property can, as they were

necessary and ordinary at the same time. Also do not forget to add your expenses for cleaning, maintenance, welcome gifts for guests, HOA fees, etc. Ask your CPA about your mortgage interest deduction and the best property investment expense there is – depreciation.

96) How can you increase your Airbnb revenue by 342 percent?

Let me tell you about one of my first properties in California. I bought it in a good location and had to choose whether I would have a long-term tenant, via a one- or two-year lease, or whether I would promote it on Airbnb for short-term rentals. Looking at the market data, if I had a long-term tenant, I would make about $1,000 a month. If it were an Airbnb, it would earn more than $3,000 a month.

The choice was: Do I go safe with a secure long-term tenant or do I go with Airbnb and earn $2,500, $3,000 or maybe more? I started thinking about the long-term lease and what would it mean. Was that so safe after all? I would be stuck with that tenant for a year or two, depending on the lease. What if they damage the place? They may not want to pay the lease or may want to leave earlier. They may want to customize the place, put artwork on the walls and damage the property in the process. They will settle in much more than the short-term guests. If short-term guests damage or change something on your property, you can just move on after their stay is over and find better guests next time. But what do you do if the long-term tenant does these things?

I realized that long-term tenant does not equal secure income and I decided to go with Airbnb. After a year, I made more than three times the revenue that I would with the long-term lease. When I looked at the revenue of all my properties and the properties of my students and compared them with the revenue from long-term leases in those specific markets I came with the number that on average Airbnb properties generate more than 342 percent more revenue than if the property would be rented with a long-term lease. This is the norm that you can see across the world, not just in the US, but also overseas.

This is one of the main drivers to choose Airbnb. You can accelerate your cash flow and make more money with the same asset. Now I look back and think why would I even want to have an asset with a long-term lease? Would that make sense? Unless the property is in a desert where absolutely nobody wants to go, only long-term tenants, it would not make sense at all. This is probably the only exception.

But Airbnb just topped seven million listings on the platform, so the message clear. There is more money to be made on Airbnb than in a regular real estate.

Chapter 9: Looking ahead to future trends and decisions

This business is always evolving to adapt to the markets and to guests' habits. Each generation brings their own expectations to any type of rental, so you must be nimble to ride the trends that come along. Airbnb started by a few friends who started renting out space to software developers on air mattresses. Look where the business has grown ever since. So, what is next? Here are some things that are on the horizon, that may be an exciting part of your future.

97) What is the office rental market potential for Airbnb?

Is Airbnb moving to the office space market? Yes, definitely.

Airbnb is striving to get into different markets. The company is currently in the luxury market with luxuryretreats.com. It is also including some boutique hotels in its listings. Airbnb Plus serves to get them more aggressively into the classic hotel business. With this expansion, they are also trying to get established in the professional business market with places for seminars, workshops, or business meetings. They have bought the company Gaest which specializes in having meetings and event spaces booked online. This is the last part of business travel to be made bookable online, now people can have their office or meeting spaces discovered and rented online. This is not a small market. It is worth $400 billion a year for the small meetings market.

However, Airbnb does have a competition in this particular market. For instance, the company Breather is already running in several big cities. It had $122 million in funding compared to the $3.5 million for Gaest, which is probably what convinced Airbnb to buy Gaest and start expanding into the office rental market under this name.

98) When will Airbnb become a publicly traded company?

Airbnb announced in 2019 that they would go for an initial public offering (IPO) in 2020. At this time, they have not said exactly what quarter. They are probably going to monitor the market very carefully to have a more precise timing in 2020.

The company has shown an exceptionally good performance. During the second quarter in 2019, its leaders have said that they made substantially more than $1 billion in revenue, for the second quarter in a row.

Not long ago, it had an evaluation of the company's value set at $31 billion in total. Those numbers are incredibly attractive, and the business is still growing. It has more than 150 million users worldwide. They are present in more than 100,000 cities.

And still it keeps growing. So, an IPO has been a long time coming.

It will be your choice if you want to own some of the stocks in Airbnb. I would caution you to be careful about the IPO. You do not want to put all your money in one basket. If you are an Airbnb host, you do not want to also have the other side of your savings in Airbnb stock. Make sure you diversify. I love it at Airbnb, but diversifying is a good idea.

We do not know yet what the valuation will be and what the IPO price will be. But the recent IPO with Uber and Lyft are now trading below the IPO price. I would be cautious putting too much money, just to own some stock of Airbnb. But you may have a wait-and-see approach when it comes to investing in Airbnb stock.

99) What is an Airbnb sabbatical?

You may have heard about new Airbnb experiences that were launched a couple of years ago. In addition to the typical Airbnb rental, they offer homes, experiences and now sabbaticals. What is sabbatical? It sounds like a great name for a vacation, but it is more than that. It gives guests a chance to volunteer for a good cause for a few weeks or have a trip with deeper meaning.

For instance, the Antarctic sabbatical is a research expedition to the most isolated place on Earth. You must apply; you cannot just pay and go. If they choose you, for four weeks you would do all kinds of important and needed research activities in Antarctica. You would work with the researchers and help to prepare their findings. Then you would spend time in Chile processing the findings with the Ocean Conservancy to become an ambassador for protecting the oceans. In that role, you will be able to share with others how they can help with minimizing the collective plastic footprint.

This is definitely a new angle for Airbnb, where you can do positive things while still using the platform. It is a great program and I hope they will do more of those. It is a great way to spend your sabbatical, if you have the time. If you are my student and rent properties as your job, you can use your free time to do something like this.

100)   What is the best exit strategy for this type of investment?

Every investor needs to think ahead and have a plan in place for a situation when it is time to sell an Airbnb investment property. While it is best to stay in this business, if you can, a situation might arise when you have no other choice but to change plans.

With an Airbnb property, the exit strategy is the same as with any other real-estate investment. You want to make sure that the equity has grown as much as possible so that you can profit as much as possible.

The location of your property is another important factor in the exit strategy. Plan ahead by investing in a neighborhood that will ensure that your property appreciates in value over time. This will help you sell any time without having to wait 30 years to be able to get your investment back.

Conclusion

Now that you have reached the end of the book, you should have enough information to start and continuously scale your Airbnb empire. You know how to look for the right properties, how to furnish, decorate, and promote them on the Airbnb listing.

You know what guests care about and what can help you make them feel at home and get you that five-star review. You also know how you can avoid some minor issues, like your guests throwing a party at your property, but also what to do if any problems do happen.

If you are, however, still hungry for more information and want to know even more about investing in Airbnb properties, be sure to check The Cash Flow Method at www.cashflowstreet.com as well as the Airbnb Investment Properties Podcast.